REFLECTIONS OF MISSOURI

Acclaim Press
— *Your Next Great Book* —

P.O. Box 238
Morley, MO 63767
(573) 472-9800
www.acclaimpress.com

Design Layout: M. Frene Melton
Cover Design: M. Frene Melton

Individual signed and numbered limited edition reproductions of the drawings in this book are available for purchase directly from the artist. Write to John Stoeckley at Reflections of Missouri, 107 S. 9th Street, Louisiana, Missouri 63353, or order directly on the website www.stoeckley.com.

Library of Congress Control Number: 2011905587

ISBN-13: 978-1-935001-74-4
ISBN-10: 1-935001-74-4

First Printing: 2011
Printed in the United States of America
10 9 8 7 6 5 4 3 2 1

REFLECTIONS OF MISSOURI

DRAWINGS AND WATERCOLORS BY

JOHN STOECKLEY

TEXT BY MARTHA SUE SMITH AND KAREN STOECKLEY

Acclaim Press
— Your Next Great Book —

Acknowledgments

Without the assistance, support and constant nagging of my lovely wife, Karen, this book may never have become a reality. Her undying confidence that a book of my work, with narrative, was something that many would enjoy and cherish, was the motivation to create this compilation of many of my works created over the last twenty years. Much of the copy found in the book is her work, through her research and commentary. Another dear friend, radio celebrity, historian and writer, Martha Sue Zuck Smith spent hundreds of hours researching and writing a great deal of the historical profiles of these images. I am profoundly thankful for her diligence and talent. Local graphic artist, Jon Moran assisted greatly in the original layout and design of the book and I thank him for this effort and support.

Henry Sweets, to whom I attribute the launching of my career as the Missouri Historian Artist, was generous in time to write a most flattering preface, and I thank him for his many years of encouragement and support. My friend and talented sculptor, Harry Weber, in whom I stand in awe of his work, was also a long time supporter and enthusiastic advocate of my career. For his most kind and humbling words I give my heartfelt thanks and appreciation.

To Doug Sikes and the entire staff at Acclaim Press, I give my deepest appreciation and thanks for their faith in my work and possibilities of this book. They are model associates for corporate ethics and honesty and they were a delight to work with. Their patience with receiving art work and copy was astounding and their warm welcome to the company was truly a unique experience.

And certainly not least, to the thousands of patrons of my work over the last twenty plus years goes a huge note of thanks. Both private and corporate collectors who have commissioned special works as well as the many folks who have my work hanging in their homes and offices, I offer my deep gratitude and thanks. Your continued support and patronage have keep me continuing to look and find new sites and images to create. To all of these people I offer my sincere gratitude.

Kansas City Region

Kansas City Region

Lakes Region

Lakes Region

Central Region

NORTHEAST REGION

St. Louis
Region

Southeast
Region

CONTENTS

ST. LOUIS REGION

SOUTHEAST REGION

FOREWORD

John Stoeckley is a draftsman and painter from the old school, where skill and feeling have equal rank. His portrayals of subjects from intimate observance of plants and birds, to the weathered wisdom of a split rail fence, to the stately grandeur of Victorian buildings, are wonderfully accurate in spirit as well as in line and shadow.

I was honored to be asked to write a few words as a foreword for this book. I have always admired the facility and precision of John's art. Each line is necessary...each one appied with the deftness of the true artist whose hand is an extension of his eye and his soul.

I have known and worked with John for well over twenty years, and continue to marvel at his passion for capturing simple scenes and life around him with the same significance he gives to monuments and famous figures. His work is art that is representative and poetic, vivid memories commited to paper.

John Stoeckley's appreciation of Missouri has helped both residents and visitors see more clearly the transcendent beauty of nature and the works of mankind throughout the state. Little known landmarks have been captured forever by John, even as they might fall into decay where they stood. John's work is from his heart, and his heart is close to Missouri and its beauties.

This book is much more than a collection of art. It is an important record of the wonders of a sometimes overlooked state, full of beauty and stories available to those who take the time to look. John Stoeckley has taken that time. He has traveled Missouri and recorded for us many of the state's hidden treasures. John shares his experiences and vision, and he teaches at the same time, through his drawing, that we don't need to venture far to find beauty and meaning. For the artist, it surrounds us every day.

Harry Weber, Sculptor
Wright City, Missouri

GATEWAY TO THE WEST

Here on the banks of the Mississippi River (St. Louis) is the Gateway Arch, a memorial to the vision of President Thomas Jefferson and to the men and women who fulfilled that westward expansion vision by exploring and settling our country west of the Mississippi River.

The Gateway Arch, designed by renowned architect Eero Saarinen, is our country's tallest monument (630 ft.) and the focal point of the Jefferson National Expansion Memorial.

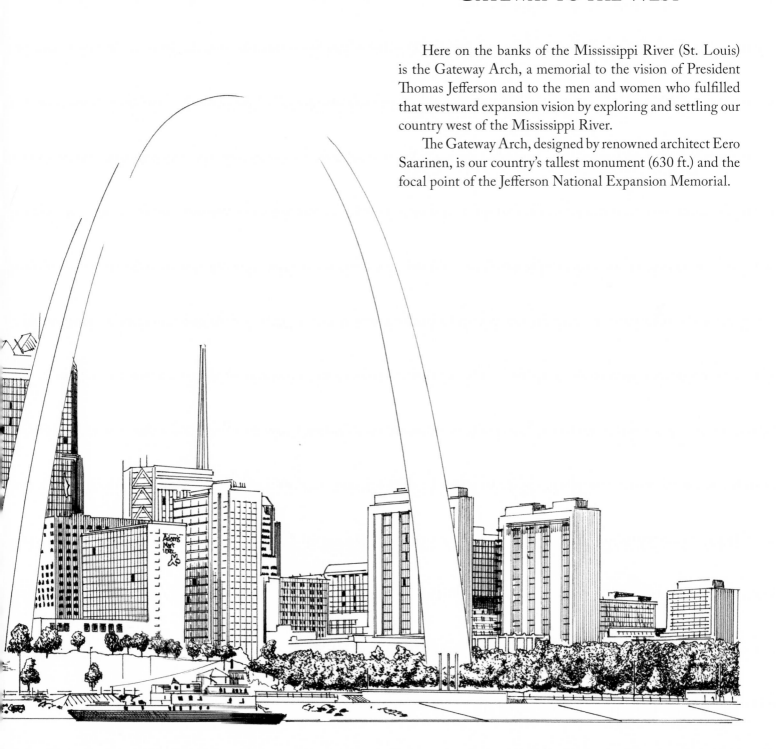

PREFACE

Many times great things come from chance meetings. This is how John Stoeckley states his career as pen and ink artist began. John credits me with his start, so let's go back to 1991 and a chance meeting.

The Mark Twain Boyhood Home was in need of major restoration work. The project was undertaken in 1990 and lasted fourteen months into May of 1991. That summer John brought his wife's automobile to Hannibal for repairs. To occupy time while awaiting the mechanic's tinkering, John wandered to the Museum Mall and began to sketch the newly restored Mark Twain Boyhood Home.

It happened that while he was sketching I ventured onto the Mall. Seeing an artist at work, I stopped and looked over his shoulder. I was impressed with the sketch he had started and we engaged in conversation. Perhaps some comment on angles was made, but John's talent and style was obvious and needed little correction or suggestion.

We stayed in touch, and as he completed the drawing the Museum offered to place reproductions on sale in the Museum store. This newly created artwork, the first to my knowledge of the newly restored Boyhood Home, sold at a brisk pace.

John found this very encouraging as this was the first historical structure drawing he had made. His mind went to work with this encouragement and he soon tackled drawing the State Capitol in Jefferson City and Busch Stadium in St. Louis. He found these also began to sell.

Before long, John had prepared enough drawings to warrant his presence in art fairs and festivals around the state. He is now a mainstay at annual shows, being asked to return by the organizing committees. In Hannibal, he is a regular at the October Historic Folklife Festival and, until its demise, the Memorial Day River Arts Festival – making more than 40 appearances at Hannibal festivals.

From his start with the Boyhood Home, John returned to Hannibal to render the Mark Twain Memorial Lighthouse, the Tom & Huck Statue and a portrait of Mark Twain in 1993, a Fence Painting Scene in 1994 and the steamboat Delta Queen passing under the Mark Twain Memorial Bridge in 1995.

The Museum and the New Era Healthcare Foundation planned a Pioneer Ball in 1996. John was approached and prepared a collage of Mark Twain related scenes tied with Mark Twain quotes on medicine. Sales of this piece helped make the ball a success.

Today, John has prepared pen and ink drawings of more than twenty buildings and statues in Hannibal. But his talent is spread across our state. He has traveled the length and breadth of Missouri capturing important public buildings, schools, churches, residences, and statues. He is forming a massive body of work that documents our culture through its structures. His pen and ink drawings number hundreds of different images.

With time, John's work has changed. He began with black and white pen and ink drawings. Then someone asked him to paint the flowers in front of a building. Next he was asked

to fully paint one of his reproductions. At shows the public flocked to his colored pieces and now the majority of his work is pen and ink with water color.

In this volume you will enjoy nearly two hundred of John's drawings, covering the state of Missouri divided into six geographical regions. If you know Missouri, you will find familiar edifices and monuments to greet you. If you are unfamiliar with our state, you will leave with a greater appreciation of Missouri's heritage as captured by one of our leading artists, John Stoeckley of Louisiana, Missouri.

I was flattered to be asked to pen a preface for John's book and stand in awe as I look at his career and future. May your pen flow unhesitatingly for many years to come as it captures and documents Missouri for the future.

Henry H. Sweets III, Curator
Mark Twain Boyhood Home and Museum
Hannibal, Missouri

ROBERT E. LEE

The *Robert E. Lee*, also known as the "Monarch of the Mississippi," made its mark in 1870 when it raced another steamboat, the *Natchez*, from New Orleans to St. Louis. The wise Captain of the *Robert E. Lee*, Captain John W. Cannon, stripped her of any excess weight and refused to take any passengers or cargo. Conversely, Captain T.P. Leathers of the *Natchez* did not feel it necessary to lighten the load. Three days, 18 hours, and 14 minutes later, the *Robert E. Lee* claimed victory over the anticipated winner, *Natchez*! The entire race was 1,278 river miles.

St. Louis Region

Bordered on the East by the Mississippi River, this region of Missouri is a wealth of history in the westward expansion of our nation. St. Louis, in and of its own, was the site of early French explorers, trappers, tradesmen and river travelers. Today, St. Louis is home to one of the most recognizable landmarks in America, if not the world. The famous "Arch" stands proudly on the banks of the Mississippi as a symbol to the great westward migration of settlers. The nearby area known as Laclede's Landing still has the cobbled streets of the early 1800s when it was a warehouse and trading area.

St. Louis is also home to the famous Anheuser Busch beer family and brewery, as well as the popular Clydesdales, their mascots. Along with this well known American beer comes sports and over the years have seen various parks and stadiums for every type of national competitive sports league.

Religion played a big role in the settling of St. Louis and the cathedrals and churches rival the architecture of its European counterparts. The mosaics in the New Cathedral Basilica are outstanding and awe inspiring to all who visit there. The Christ Church Cathedral reflects the Anglican influence of early church architecture.

From the Botanical Gardens to the Butterfly House, there is plenty of nature to visit and enjoy in the area. Forest Park, and many other neighborhood parks offer respite from the hustle and bustle of city life.

The higher education opportunities in the region are depicted through John's depiction of important campus buildings. Many stand the test of time and boast various famous people having passed through their portals and through their education.

The region crosses the Missouri River to St. Charles, the starting point of the famous Lewis & Clark Expedition. Extending even farther west to the cliffs along the Missouri river to St. Albans, one can discover a totally different topography and points of interest. Then traveling south to the densely German populated areas of Marthasville, Washington and Hermann, you can see the influence of the immigrants in the business names along the downtown streets. These towns along the Missouri River are home to various wineries, the pride of Missouri in the award winning wines they produce.

Further south along the Mississippi River is the oldest French settled town west of the Mississippi, Ste. Genevieve, where very early examples of French architecture still stand today. John's drawings depict the vertical pole building system used by these earliest settlers as well as later brick buildings built from ballast of French trading ships.

This region offers much to artist, traveler and historian alike.

Statue of Saint Louis

Entrance to the St. Louis Art Museum

The statue of Saint Louis, King Louis IX of France, stands at the entrance to the St. Louis Art Museum. Pierre Laclede named the village he founded "Saint Louis" in 1764 in honor of the reigning French King Louis XV, whose patron saint was Louis IX. It was the symbol of the city until the Gateway Arch was built. The original plaster model of the statue stood at the main entrance to the 1904 World's Fair.

Arch From Laclede's Landing

Two of the most familiar Missouri sites are depicted here, the St. Louis Gateway Arch as seen from Laclede's Landing. In 1763, two French fur trappers set out from New Orleans for the purpose of establishing a more northern trading post along the Mississippi River. Pierre Laclede chose the west bank of the river, just north of the River des Peres and south of the Missouri River. By 1784, the trading post had become a sizable port and trade area and Laclede named the settlement St. Louis in honor of the patron saint of the King of France.

Today, Laclede's Landing is a nine-block stretch of unique restaurants, sidewalk cafes, and specialty shops all enticing you with their contained history along the cobblestone streets.

OLD COURTHOUSE

St. Louis

The Old Courthouse and the Gateway Arch, part of the Jefferson National Expansion Memorial, are St. Louis' oldest and newest landmarks.

Construction of the courthouse began in 1839, and was expanded and modified many times until completion of the present dome in 1862. It was a vital part of the city's history and became nationally known during the famous Dred Scott trial. The original murals, courtrooms and historic exhibits of St. Louis will delight any visitor.

The Arch, St. Louis' "Gateway to the West" is a modern engineering achievement, with its exciting ride to the top for a superb view of the St. Louis skyline.

Laclede's Landing

In 1763, two French fur trappers set out from New Orleans for the purpose of establishing a trading post. Pierre Laclede chose the west bank of the Mississippi River, north of the River des Peres and south of the Missouri River. In 1784, Laclede named the settlement St. Louis in honor of the patron saint of the king of France.

This nine square block of renovated 100-year-old warehouse buildings was the heart of St. Louis' river commerce in the 1800s. Great river boats and barges arrived and departed the adjacent riverfront, bringing wares from all over the world and hauling away grain and other agricultural products. The restored buildings in the Laclede's Landing area offer interesting shopping, fine dining and entertainment along original cobblestone streets, just a short walk from the Jefferson National Expansion Memorial Arch.

Clydesdales

Anheuser-Busch, a St. Louis icon and the home of Budweiser Beer, self-endorsed as the "King of Beers," boasts the Clydesdales as the "King of Horses." The Clydesdales are the beverage industry's most recognizable mascots. August A. Busch, Jr. presented his father with a six-horse hitch of Clydesdales in celebration of the repeal of Prohibition in 1933.

The Clydesdale breed itself hails from Clydesdale, Scotland. They are capable of extremely hard work yet exude grace and beauty. One of their most discernible traits is the long hair that falls from just below the horses' knees and hocks, covering the hooves.

OLD ARENA

Lovingly referred to as the "Old Barn," the St. Louis Arena, whose roof resembled the back of a humpbacked whale, was built in 1929. It had a seating capacity of nearly 20,000 and was considered the most modern and complete sports facility in the United States! Its original purpose, however, was to be host of the National Dairy Exposition. It later became the home of the St. Louis Blues, and one might have attended indoor circuses, horse shows, prize fights, conventions, and various other exhibits.

The "Old Barn" withstood, with some damage, a tornado in the 1950s and had begun to fall apart due to the lack of upkeep. However, once the St. Louis Blues were purchased around 1968, the St. Louis Arena began its ongoing renovation. Ralston Purina purchased the St. Louis Blues and the "Old Barn" and changed the name to "The Checkerdome." It was demolished on February 27, 1999.

UNION STATION

In 1883, the first corner stone of St. Louis Union Station was laid to the exacting specifications of architect Theodore Link. This magnificent structure was modeled after a medieval city in southern France, Carcassonne. The structure was completed in September 1894 and became the busiest train station in the United States, servicing over 100,000 passengers each day between 1904 and 1940. In 1976, the station was placed on the National Register of Historical Places and the last train pulled out of the station in October 1978.

Today, Union Station has been restored to its original grand atmosphere and once again is a link between the East and the West as a mixed use entertainment center, offering travelers and local folks hotel accommodations, specialty shops, restaurants, concerts by the lake, live comedy and great entertainment throughout the year.

BUSCH MEMORIAL STADIUM

Busch Memorial Stadium was demolished by wrecking ball on December 8, 2005. In 1964, ground was broken for Busch Stadium and it soon officially opened as the new home of the St. Louis Cardinals. Busch Stadium was the vision of August A. Busch Jr., and this vision became a reality and was the catalyst for the renovation and redevelopment of downtown St. Louis.

Civic Center Busch Memorial Stadium was the original name of the stadium until December 31, 1981, when it was renamed Busch Memorial Stadium (or Busch Stadium). The stadium was originally designed for the sport of baseball only, but was later redesigned to include football.

Note: The playing field of Busch Stadium was 10 to 30 feet lower than the street level. To have reached seating in the stadium, you had to either go up or down from one of its eight major entrances.

"...HERE STANDS
BASEBALL'S PERFECT WARRIOR
...HERE STANDS
BASEBALL'S PERFECT KNIGHT"

BUSCH STADIUM

New Busch Stadium

"Batter up!" That's the way you feel when you see an aerial view of the beautifully modern "new" Busch Stadium in St. Louis! With a seating capacity of 46,861, a view of the Gateway Arch, a view of the downtown St. Louis skyline, and knowing the Cardinals will be playing, what more could a baseball fan ask? Don't be at all maudlin about the loss of the "old" stadium, because the "new" Busch Stadium shares some of the "old" site it replaced. When you attend a baseball game in the new stadium, completed in 2006, you get all the excitement and thrill you hope for when attending a professional sports event.

Musial Statue

There is not a simple answer to why is there a statue of Stan Musial at Busch Stadium. No, there are many reasons, starting, no doubt, with some facts about "Stan the Man." His entire professional baseball career was with the St. Louis Cardinals (1941-1963). He is considered the Cardinals' greatest player, maybe because he was recognized as a remarkable hitter and maybe because the Cardinals became a "perennial power-house" with Musial's batting. The "Man" led the National League in hitting seven times! Even at age 41, he said, "I was having too much fun hitting to want to quit." He had 475 home runs in his 22-year career with the Cardinals. Maybe his statue stands at Busch Stadium because, even after his retirement, he was still a popular figure in St. Louis, running his restaurant and speaking often. Musial also served one year as general manager of the Cardinals. He was very gracious and unassuming, actually somewhat shy, and extremely gentlemanly, modest, and down-to-earth. "Stan the Man" was elected to the National Baseball Hall of Fame in 1969, his first year of eligibility, and inducted into the St. Louis Walk of Fame in 1989. The Cardinals retired Musial's uniform number "6" at the end of the 1963 season. Yes, there definitely is not just one single reason Stanislaus Musial's statue stands proudly at Busch Stadium in St. Louis.

CATHEDRAL BASILICA OF ST. LOUIS

Replacing the Church of St. Louis IX (aka the Old Cathedral) in the early 20th century, the new Cathedral contains 83,000 square feet of mosaic murals, the world's largest collection of mural mosaics. The beauty and grandeur of this Cathedral rivals any European church or cathedral.

As you leave the cathedral, notice on the front lawn the Angel of Harmony, a sculpture 14 feet in height intended to "emphasize the theme of harmony, peace and racial justice" according to Auxiliary Bishop Edward Braxton.

THE OLD CATHEDRAL

St. Louis' historic Old Cathedral, known officially as the Basilica of St. Louis, the King, is one of the world's most honored churches. It stands on a tiny plot, the only building on the Jefferson National Expansion Memorial, on the downtown riverfront. It was on this plot, now shaded by the soaring Gateway Arch, that the first Mass was celebrated in St. Louis in 1764.

Over 200 years ago in 1770, the first log chapel was dedicated and the parish was founded. The second church was built in 1776, also of logs, and served as a cathedral for Bishop DuBourg until the brick church was dedicated in 1820. A second dedication took place on October 26, 1837, when final work was completed under the direction of Bishop Joseph Rosati. The most important honor ever afforded any American church was handed down in 1961 by His Holiness, the late Pope John XXIII, who decreed Basilican status upon the church.

SPORTSMAN'S PARK

The all-time home run leader at Sportsman's Park was Stan Musial with 252. The all-time home run leader at Sportsman's Park as a visitor was Babe Ruth with 58. Sportsman's Park was the site of the 1940, 1948, and 1957 All-Star games.

Statistics, statistics, statistics – but isn't that an important part of baseball? Sportsman's Park certainly had its share of statistics, records, and history.

1866: Baseball at the original site. 1875: The Brown Stockings played. 1880: Alfred Spink bought the team and tore down the ballpark. 1881: Covered Sportsman's Park opened.

1891: Sportsman's Park burned. 1892: Browns were renamed the Cardinals. 1898: Sportsman's Park burned again. 1901: St. Louis Browns formed. 1908: St. Louis Browns built a new ballpark where Sportsman's Park burned in 1898. 1920: Sam Breadon (owner of the Cardinals) sold the ballpark, Cardinals moved to Sportsman's Park. 1940: First night game under lights at Sportsman's Park. 1953: Browns move to Baltimore – Sportsman's Park renamed Busch Stadium. 1966: Last game played at Sportsman's Park. Days later Cardinals moved into Busch Memorial Stadium.

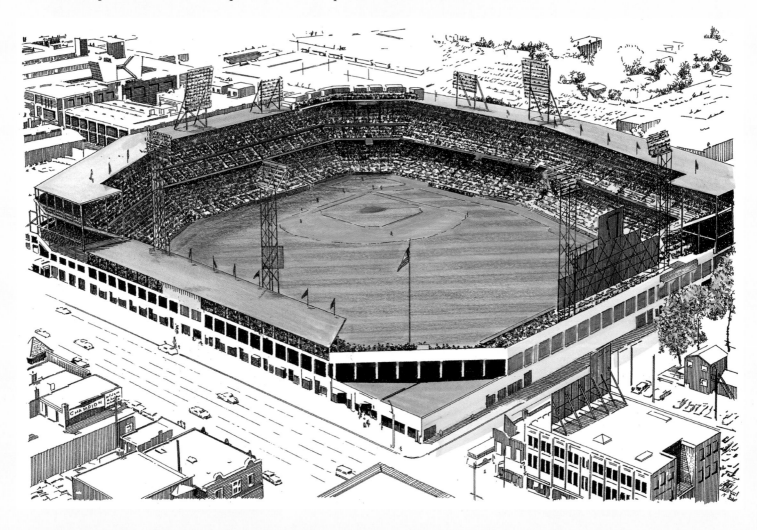

Fox Theatre

William Fox opened the "new" theatre in St. Louis on January 31, 1929. From that point on, W.F., as he was nicknamed, took the Fox Theatre to the top of the industry, both in entertainment and in dollars. W.F. was in a tragic auto accident the same year he opened the Fox Theatre. He was seriously injured, but yet another crash ensued – the crash of the Stock Market – and W.F. was trapped in a $91,000,000 debt. He died in 1952, having financially recovered, but he was "never able to re-establish his entertainment empire and died the film industry's forgotten man."

William Fox's wife, Eve Leo, decorated and furnished the theatre. Mrs. Fox traveled the world purchasing pieces of art, sculptures, and furnishings. A splendid chandelier, 13 feet in diameter, weighing 2,000 pounds enhanced by 1,244 pieces of jeweled glass and 159 light bulbs, was restored and is suspended from the dome of the auditorium. The lobby is every bit as dazzling with "lions and sea monsters," rows of flanking columns, and a grand staircase.

Situated in the arts district in midtown St. Louis, the Fox Theatre has a bright future as it continues to offer splendid entertainment.

CHRIST CHURCH CATHEDRAL

Christ Church in St. Louis, now a National Historic Landmark, became Christ Church Cathedral for the Episcopal Diocese of Missouri in June 1880. However, Christ Church Cathedral continues to serve as a parish in addition to being the cathedral. In the 1960s, the chapel was completely remodeled and other restorations made. This drawing was presented to Bishop Desmond TuTu during his visit to the cathedral by John's father-in-law, Roger Kramer, then a lay reader at Calvary Church, Louisiana.

CIVIL COURTS BUILDING

St. Louis

The Civil Courts Building in St. Louis was dedicated and occupied on June 21, 1930. The building resembles a Greek temple in appearance. The architectural staff of the City of St. Louis Plaza Commission designed the building.

St. Ambrose Roman Catholic Church

St. Ambrose Roman Catholic Church plays an enormous part in the area of St. Louis known as the "Hill." The majority of residents of the "Hill" are Italian Americans. With the immigration of Italian heritage, so came the influence of the Roman Catholic Church.

The Parish of St. Ambrose was founded in 1903. That frame structure burned and the new Church of St. Ambrose was built in 1926. It is modeled after Sant'Ambrogio Church in Milan. St. Ambrose Roman Catholic Church is a landmark in the community. "The Italian Immigrants" is a statue that stands in front of St. Ambrose Church, portraying the immigrant families that settled in the neighborhood fondly known as the "Hill."

Compton Hill Water Tower

One of seven remaining water towers in the United States is the Compton Hill Water Tower in St. Louis. The Compton Hill Water Tower was built in 1898, camouflaging the 100-foot tall standpipe. Housed in the top of the tower is an observation deck boasting a 360-degree view of St. Louis. The Compton Hill Water Tower was retired in 1929, but was renovated in 1999. The Compton Hill/Reservoir Square Neighborhood Association offers tours of the tower on a non-regular basis.

In 1966, the Compton Hill Water Tower was declared a city landmark and it was added to the National Register of Historic Places in 1972.

CLIMATRON CONSERVATORY

The Climatron Conservatory is an integral part of Missouri Botanical Garden in St. Louis. The structure of the Climatron is amazing in that it has no interior support – no columns from floor to ceiling. It was developed by two St. Louis architects, Murphy and Mackey, and won the 1961 Reynolds Award for "architectural excellence in aluminum." This honor was due, in part, to the fact that the original outer structure was made of lightweight aluminum. The structure has been awarded honors such as being named one of the 100 most significant architectural achievements in United States history.

The Climatron dome, as it stands today following its renovation in 1988, is a dome within a dome. The original structure was kept in place due to its uniqueness, remembering that it was the world's first geodesic dome greenhouse. There are over 1,200 species of plants in the Climatron Conservatory.

JEWEL BOX

In 1936, the city of St. Louis built the floral conservatory, the Jewel Box. Remarkably designed, it looks as if you could take giant steps up to the roof; it is cantilevered, with vertical glass walls reaching 50 feet high using 15,000 square feet of glass. A significant part of Forest Park, the Jewel Box sits on a 17-acre site. The conservatory is listed on the National Register of Historic Places.

Permanent displays of perennial plants and seasonal displays of annual plants and flowers grace the Jewel Box.

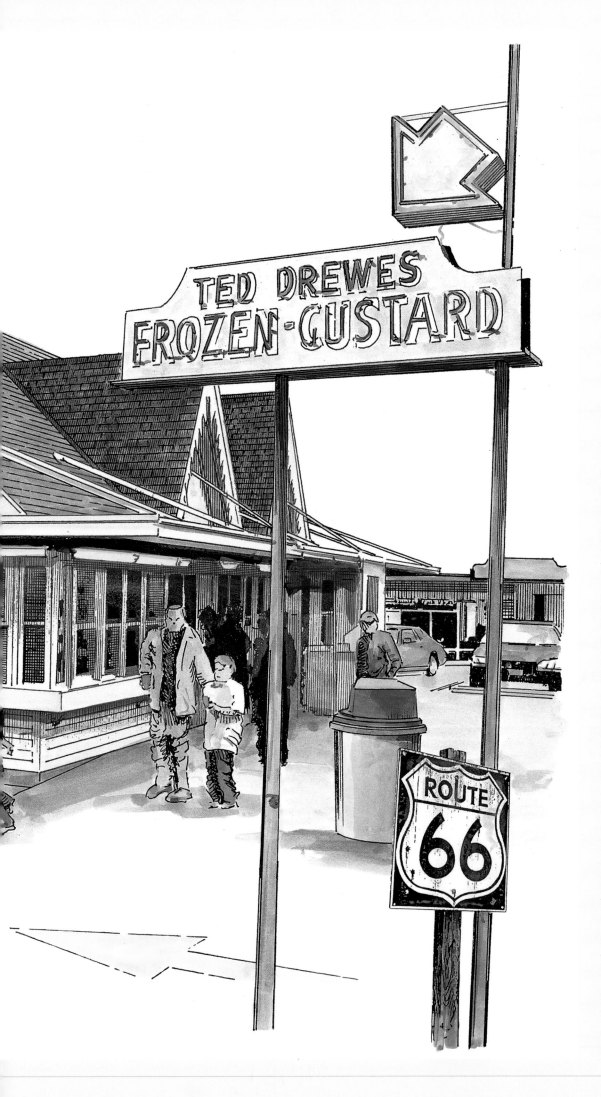

TED DREWES

Ted Drewes has been selling ice cream, or frozen custard as St. Louis folks know it, since 1929 when he opened his first stand in Florida. Remember, that year was the beginning of the Great Depression, and ice cream was a novelty to many. In 1930, Ted opened another store on Natural Bridge Road in St. Louis and then another in 1931 on South Grand. Moving on to 1941, the stand was opened at the Chippewa location on old Route 66. It still stands today as a St. Louis icon. Ted attributes his long time success to quality and consistency. Folks stand in long lines to get the famous custard, knowing it is worth the wait. After John finished this commission drawing of the stand, Ted and his wife traveled to Louisiana to receive the original drawing, leaving coupons for John to receive free custard. It just doesn't get any better!

St. Louis University High School

Since 1818, St. Louis University High School has been a Latin school for boys, first known as St. Louis Academy, then St. Louis College, and finally St. Louis University High School. The high school is a Jesuit Catholic high school for boys. It is the oldest secondary educational institution in the United States west of the Mississippi River, and one of the largest private high schools in Missouri.

ST. LOUIS UNIVERSITY HIGH SCHOOL

CHRISTIAN BROTHERS COLLEGE HIGH SCHOOL

Christian Brothers College High School was founded in St. Louis in 1850; however, the "story" goes much farther back in history than that. The Brothers of the Christian Schools, which happens to be in 80 countries, established itself over 320 years ago when Saint John Baptist de La Salle, a French priest, saw the need for a group of laymen who would dedicate their lives to the ministry of Christian education. Christian Brothers College High School utilizes the spirituality of Saint John Baptist de La Salle, "Lasallian spirituality." Christian Brothers

College High School is a private, all-male secondary school with Catholic and Lasallian affiliation.

The purpose of this institute is to give a human and Christian education to the young, especially the poor, according to the ministry which the church has entrusted to it. The motto of Christian Brothers College High School is "Religion, morals, culture," which is a major order carried out at Christian Brothers College High School.

BROOKINGS HALL

Washington University

Brookings Hall is an integral structure on the campus of Washington University in St. Louis. The building was completed in 1902, originally named University Hall and used as an administrative center. It was designed by James P. Jamieson, who was a representative of the Philadelphia firm Cope & Stewardson. Interestingly, a similar building – Blair Hall – was designed by the same firm in 1897 on the campus of Princeton University.

Robert S. Brookings became a successful St. Louis businessman, along with his brother, in the company Cupples & Marston, a woodenware and willowware wholesale business. Robert Brookings contributed $200,000 to Washington University for the construction of an administrative building. He was a member of the University's Board of Directors and served as president from 1895 to 1928. University Hall was renamed Brookings Hall on June 12, 1928, in honor of board president Robert S. Brookings. Administrative offices are currently housed in Brookings Hall.

GRAHAM CHAPEL

Washington University

Graham Chapel is nestled on the Hilltop Campus of Washington University, which is a National Historic Landmark. Named for her deceased husband, Benjamin Brown Graham, Christine Blair Graham gave the chapel to the university. Benjamin Brown Graham died in 1904 and Graham Chapel was dedicated in 1909.

Clock Tower/Cupples House

Saint Louis University

Saint Louis University is the oldest university west of the Mississippi River and the second-oldest Jesuit College in the nation. This clock tower, as well as the Cupples House, is located in the center of the campus.

The Cupples House was originally owned by Samuel Cupples, but was named the Chouteau House after Charles Chouteau, the first student enrolled at Saint Louis University under the Jesuit administration. However, in 1970 the name was changed back from Chouteau House to Cupples House. The house has 42 rooms, 22 fireplaces, and truly a mansion now housing educational exhibitions and art exhibits. The university has one of the largest glass collections in the midwest and this, too, is housed in the Cupples House. Both the tower and the house are listed on the National Register of Historic Places.

BILLIKEN

A favorite story about the joining of the Billiken and Saint Louis University is an obituary in 1946 that recorded the death of Billy Gunn. Gunn owned a drug store near the university and had become friends with the university's athletes and coaches. Coach Bender, SLU's football coach was in Gunn's drug store one day and he greeted the Coach, "Bender, you're a real Billiken!" A sports writer, William O'Conner, overheard the remark. The name for Coach Bender stuck and the university's mascot became the Billiken!

Another story points out that Coach Bender resembled the Billiken. A caricature of Bender was drawn and placed in the window of a drug store, and the football team soon became known as Bender's Billikens.

SAINT FRANCIS XAVIER COLLEGE CHURCH
Saint Louis University

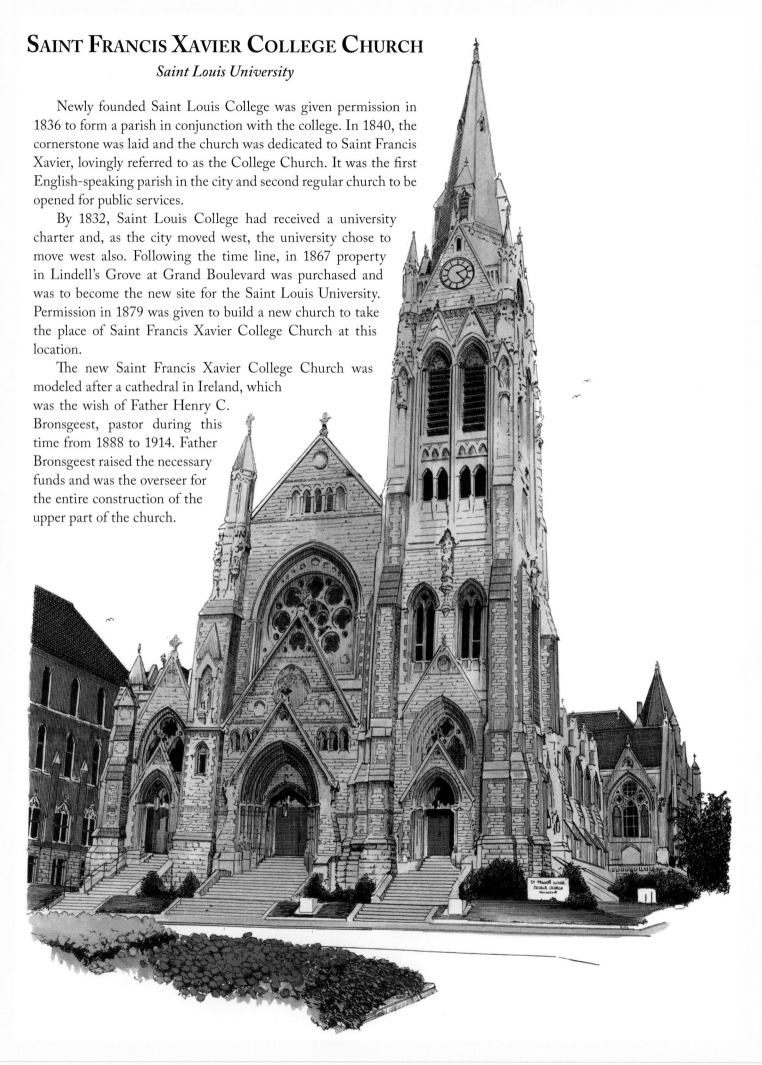

Newly founded Saint Louis College was given permission in 1836 to form a parish in conjunction with the college. In 1840, the cornerstone was laid and the church was dedicated to Saint Francis Xavier, lovingly referred to as the College Church. It was the first English-speaking parish in the city and second regular church to be opened for public services.

By 1832, Saint Louis College had received a university charter and, as the city moved west, the university chose to move west also. Following the time line, in 1867 property in Lindell's Grove at Grand Boulevard was purchased and was to become the new site for the Saint Louis University. Permission in 1879 was given to build a new church to take the place of Saint Francis Xavier College Church at this location.

The new Saint Francis Xavier College Church was modeled after a cathedral in Ireland, which was the wish of Father Henry C. Bronsgeest, pastor during this time from 1888 to 1914. Father Bronsgeest raised the necessary funds and was the overseer for the entire construction of the upper part of the church.

Saint Louis University Medical School

Continuing the excellence in education, the medical school, which is a part of Saint Louis University, is a leader in research in many fields, especially in emerging diseases and afflictions of the liver.

Saint Louis University Medical Department was established in 1836 and had the distinction, in 1839, of awarding the first M.D. degree granted west of the Mississippi River. Due to troubled times, in 1854 the university's Medical Department separated from the university. For 59 years, Saint Louis University was without a medical school.

Under the leadership of President Father William Banks Rogers (1900-1908), Saint Louis University trustees approved the integration of a new medical school into the university. President Rogers was able to raise funds to purchase Marion Sims-Beaumont College of Medicine, and in 1903 the purchase was consummated. Today, Saint Louis University School of Medicine is one of eleven schools within the University.

SAINT LOUIS COLLEGE OF PHARMACY

The Saint Louis College of Pharmacy is a private and independent nonsectarian campus. It is the oldest college of pharmacy west of the Mississippi River, having been founded in 1864. Saint Louis College of Pharmacy is highly respected in the medical community. Not only is the college one of the largest colleges of pharmacy in America, it is also one of the few that has remained independent and has not become a part of a larger university.

Fontbonne University

Fontbonne University is located in suburban St. Louis. After the French Revolution, Mother St. John Fontbonne refounded the congregation of the Sisters of St. Joseph. Some 28 years later, six sisters of St. Joseph settled in the United States in Carondelet.

In 1841, those sisters opened St. Joseph's Academy for girls. The Fontbonne Academy was then opened at that site, and the first college level classes were held in 1923. Two years later, the Academy, now Fontbonne College, was moved to Clayton.

Fontbonne College changed its academic status and became Fontbonne University in 2002. The university is a private, Catholic, four-year, coed, liberal arts institution offering both undergraduate and master's degrees. A unique program offered at Fontbonne University is its nationally known Deaf Education major.

WEBSTER UNIVERSITY

Webster University grew locally, beginning with five students in 1915, to what it is today, operating more than 100 locations around the world. Some of Webster University campuses are in Switzerland, Austria, England, and other countries as well.

Webster University was one of the first Catholic women's colleges west of the Mississippi River. It was not until late in the 1960s the university was fully coeducational.

The "home campus" of Webster University remains in Webster Groves, Missouri, and excellence in education remains its primary purpose.

The youngest son of John Stoeckley, Clark, is a recipient of the Daniel Webster four-year scholarship and a graduate from the Leigh Gerdine College of Fine Arts.

MARYVILLE UNIVERSITY

Maryville University is proud to be one of the oldest private institutions in the St. Louis region. It was founded in 1872 and was originally an academy for women. Maryville University became a four-year college, became co-educational, and then a university in 1991.

Another change took place one hundred years after being founded, in 1972, when ownership of the college was transferred from the Religious of the Sacred Heart to a lay board of trustees.

Maryville University was the first school in the St. Louis area to introduce non-traditional educational opportunities by offering weekend classes, alternate evening classes, and now online classes, continuing education classes, and other services to accommodate students.

LOGAN COLLEGE OF CHIROPRACTIC

Seven young men and women made up the first class of Logan College of Chiropractic on September 1, 1935. Since that time, Logan College of Chiropractic has grown, as has its campus. It is now the third largest chiropractic college or university among 43 worldwide.

The college was named for Hugh B. Logan, D.C., its founder and first president. Dr. Hugh Logan died in 1944 and his son took the reigns; under his leadership Logan College of Chiropractic continued its expansion. Today, an expanded 112-acre campus is located in Chesterfield, Missouri.

St. Charles Depot

Until 1986, the Missouri-Kansas-Texas rail line traveled its route from Machens in St. Charles County to Sedalia in Pettis County. For almost 100 years the St. Charles Depot was a hub. The depot was built in 1892, and the first train on the Missouri-Kansas-Texas (KATY for short) passed through St. Charles in 1894. The last passenger train stopped at the depot in 1958.

The St. Charles Depot, a 55-ton building with all its history and memories, was moved in 1976 to its present location in Frontier Park in St. Charles.

FIRST STATE CAPITOL

On November 25, 1820, Governor Alexander McNair signed a bill making St. Charles the first capital of Missouri. Missouri's first legislators – some frontiersmen and others of the gentry – met in this building from June 1821 through October 1826 to undertake the task of reorganizing Missouri's territorial government into a progressive state system.

BLANCHETTE CHOUTEAU MILL
1769

Originally this grist mill was log construction much like a cabin. Over the years it was enlarged until it looked like this in 1850. At first it was a water-powered grist mill and later became a steam-powered woolen mill. During the Civil War, the Union Army confiscated the mill and turned out woolen blankets and mittens for the soldiers. Rumor has it that the Lewis and Clark Expedition set out on the first leg of their journey from the mill. The mill is located in St. Charles and now is the home of "Trailhead Brewing Co.," a restaurant and microbrewery.

LEWIS & CLARK CENTER
St. Charles

Along the Missouri River in historic St. Charles stands the Lewis & Clark Center, a museum and trading post devoted to discovering and learning America's rich history and culture.

As a certified site on the Lewis and Clark Trail, the Lewis & Clark Center depicts the expedition from their rendezvous in St. Charles, through the Louisiana Territory, across the Rocky Mountains, all the way to the Pacific Ocean.

Visitors are invited to share in this amazing exploration that triggered the opening of the west.

SACRED HEART ACADEMY
St. Charles

The Academy of the Sacred Heart is a member of the National Catholic Educational Association. There are over 138 Schools of the Sacred Heart in the world, all adhering to the same philosophy: "Goals of Sacred Heart Education: Faith, Intellectual Values, Social Action, Community and Personal Growth."

Sacred Heart Academy in St. Charles is an independent, private, co-ed Catholic elementary school. The School was founded in 1818 and has a meaningful history. St. Philippine Duchesne opened the first free school west of the Mississippi

River. The oldest part of the school is open to visitors. Wrapped deeply with history, housed within are beautiful statues, shrines, mosaics, stained glass windows, and relics of the pioneer convent are on exhibit.

Great pride is taken in the way the academy continues to enlarge its facilities throughout its long history dating back to 1835. Learning "to base their conviction solidly on Christian values in order to effect social transformation and meaningful growth" continues to be taught at Sacred Heart Academy.

STUDIO AT ST. ALBANS

In the early 1920s, the Johnson family of St. Louis was seeking the perfect place to build their majestic "home," which by today's standards would be considered a castle. The Johnsons commissioned Theodore Link, the architect of St. Louis Union Station, to design their home. Link designed the Studio on a hillside overlooking the Missouri River and the beautiful St. Albans valley.

PEACE CHAPEL
Daniel Boone Home

The Peace Chapel, now in Defiance, demonstrates the strength of some buildings. Peace Chapel not only has had several moves, but also has served many purposes, such as a general store, dance hall, and finally a church. Before moving to Definace, the Peace Chapel was originally built in New Melle in the mid-1800s.

THE DANIEL BOONE HOME

America's most famous pioneer began building this home in 1802 resembling his birthplace in Pennsylvania and ancestral Boone residences in Devon, England.

The four-story Georgian-style structure has been faithfully restored and furnished with furniture of that period, much from the belongings of Daniel and his relatives.

The home, located 35 miles west of St. Louis, was built on his son Nathan's tract of land, which Daniel had given to his son. Daniel lived in this house until his death in 1820.

EBENEZER UNITED CHURCH OF CHRIST

Augusta

Ebenezer United Church of Christ is a beautiful, small church established in Augusta, Missouri by German immigrants in 1851. Augusta wasn't incorporated until 1855, but it had all ready become a successful agricultural community. In addition to grain and livestock, wine grapes flourished. Originally the church was named Evangelische Ebenezer Kirche, reflecting the congregation and their German language. In the mid-1900s, the name was changed to its present name, demonstrating the congregations philosophy of "deep roots yet modern thinking."

MOUNT PLEASANT WINERY

Augusta

In 1859, the Mount Pleasant Winery was founded in Augusta, Missouri, atop the beautiful Missouri hills, which resembled in climate and terrain the best wine-producing regions in Germany. Georg and Fredrick Munch, who founded Mount Pleasant Winery, found that the Augusta area reminded them of their homeland, and therefore they felt would prove to be the suitable place for their winery. Using Augusta limestone with handmade bricks manufactured on the property, the two built the Mount Pleasant Winery.

The vineyards were destroyed because of Prohibition, and the business of winemaking in the region ended. However, 40 years later, vineyards were planted and using the original cellars, the varietals of Missouri were once again cultivated. Since that time, Mount Pleasant Winery has produced award-winning wines.

Montauk Mill

The Montauk Mill is located in Montauk State Park, near Salem. Erected in 1896, Montauk Mill was capable of producing both "patent" flour (white) and "common" flour (whole wheat). Corn grinding stones were used to grind corn to make cornmeal and feed for livestock. The corn grinding stones were imported from France and were a unique porous flint rock. The mill was turbine powered.

Montauk Mill was built as part of the early settlers' establishment of a self-sufficient community in the early 1800s.

The mill had elaborate milling machinery and much of it is still in place. It was constructed with native shortleaf pine and oak hardwoods, which were harvested from the surrounding area. The mill is the only remaining structure of the once-thriving Montauk community.

Montauk State Park boasts some of the finest trout fishing in the Midwest and the Montauk Mill is an historic site, proudly standing over 100 years.

Gasconade County Courthouse

Hermann

The first Gasconade County Seat was in Gasconade City; however, due to frequent flooding of the Gasconade River flooding the courthouse in Gasconade City, the county seat was moved to Bartonville, which is also on the Gasconade River and was swallowed by flooding water. Mt. Sterling was the number three location of the Gasconade County Seat. In 1842, a vote of the county was taken and the Gasconade County Seat was determined to move to Hermann.

A courthouse was built in Hermann, and Daniel M. Boone, son of the famous Daniel Boone, was appointed one of the commissioners of the Territorial Legislature. Mr. Boone also served as one of the first justices of the Gasconade County Court.

The courthouse that stands today was a gift to the county by a local Hermann merchant, Charles D. Eitzen, and was built in 1896-1898 and is probably the only privately gifted courthouse in the United States. A fire in 1905 did some damage to the building, but the damage was repaired and continues to undergo restoration.

HERMANNHOF WINERY

Missouri has had a strong influence in the wine industry of the world, purportedly saving the French wine industry in the late 1800s from a root stock blight that nearly destroyed the French vines. Hermannhof Winery, with a proud German heritage dating back to 1852, was part of the supply of healthy root stock shipped to France. The winery, listed as a National Historical Site, is located close to the Missouri River in the town of Hermann.

STONE HILL WINERY

Stone Hill Winery was established in 1847; however, Prohibition in 1920 devastated the wine industry in Missouri. During Prohibition, the winery's underground cellars, which are said to be "the largest series of vaulted cellars in America," were used to raise mushrooms.

Jim and Betty Held purchased the winery in 1965. After restoring the cellars and beautiful buildings, the Helds can boast that Stone Hill Winery is Missouri's oldest and most awarded winery. Stone Hill Winery is known internationally as well as nationally.

Meramec Caverns Barn

Stanton

"Get your kicks on Route 66," was the phrase that affectionately referred to Route 66 as the mother road. Some of the "kicks" you'll get while driving this scenic road are the Meramec Caverns barn murals. The existing barn murals are generally "grandfathered" under the laws in most states that prohibit any new barn murals. Fortunately, some have been restored and are still being enjoyed even today.

Lester B. Dill, owner of the Meramec Caverns, was the main promoter of these murals, offering to paint the barns for free if the farmers would permit the murals.

SANDY CREEK
COVERED BRIDGE

Sandy Creek Covered Bridge was constructed in 1872 in Jefferson County as part of a county-wide building program following the Civil War. John H. Morse proposed spanning Sandy Creek with a wood-covered bridge 74 feet, 6 inches long and 18 feet, 10 inches wide, with an entrance height of 13 feet. The bridge was built on the Hillsboro and Lemay Ferry gravel road connecting Hillsboro and St. Louis. Destroyed by flood in May 1886, it was rebuilt by Henry Steffin to the original specifications using some of the original timbers and abutments.

JEAN BAPTISTE BEQUETTE HOUSE

Ste. Genevieve

Not only is Ste. Genevieve one of the most historical settlements in the state of Missouri, it also has some extremely historical homes dating back to the early-to-mid-1700s. The Jean Baptiste Bequette House, circa 1780, is one of these homes. Because of the historical significance surrounding Ste. Genevieve, it has been designated a National Landmark Historic District.

Ste. Genevieve was originally settled on the west bank of the Mississippi River by French Canadians. A devastating flood occurred in 1785, forcing Ste. Genevieve inhabitants to move about three miles from the original site to its present location. The settlement changed hands several times between the Spanish and the French, and finally Emperor Napoleon sold it with the Louisiana Purchase to the United States in 1803.

SAINTE GENEVIEVE CATHOLIC CHURCH

French Catholic Canadians settled near the present location of Ste. Genevieve, and the name Ste. Genevieve alone displays the Catholic influence. The town is named after Sainte Genevieve, "the patron saint of Paris." In 1803, the Louisiana Purchase made Ste. Genevieve part of the United States.

With its Catholic history, the beautiful Sainte Genevieve Catholic Church reflects the multiple heritages it has embraced. Its cornerstone was laid in 1876 and the "14-foot cross was placed atop the steeple on November 1, 1879. It stands on the site of the original log church believed to have been built circa 1754." A stone church was erected in 1837 replacing the log structure, and the church as it stands today was built around that stone structure. Ste. Genevieve is the oldest permanent settlement in Missouri.

FELIX VALLE HOUSE

There are certain charms about the style of historic homes that show the pioneer spirit of early settlers. Such is the fascination in touring the period-furnished museum house in Ste. Genevieve, Missouri, the Felix Valle House! Jacob Philipson built this house using native limestone in 1818, and in 1824 Jean Baptiste Valle purchased it. His son, Felix, bought the house from his father in 1835. The Valle House is in the National Historic Landmark District and is open to the public. As you tour the house, keep in mind you are stepping back into the Federal style of the 1800s, a piece of Missouri's French colonial past.

The Old Brick

Located in Ste. Genevieve, Missouri, this building was built by John Price in 1780 and is heralded as the oldest brick building west of the Mississippi River. This structure was originally designed to house a store and ferry boat operation, but later sold to satisfy debts of Mr. Price.

Tradition reports that the house was constructed from bricks brought from France in ships using them as ballast. From 1804 to 1809, this building was the first Territorial Court Building.

THE SOUTHERN HOTEL

The Southern Hotel is located in Ste. Genevieve, Missouri. Originally, the Southern Hotel was built in the 1790s as a private home. It began to operate as a hotel in 1805 and today operates as a Bed & Breakfast.

Some of the claims of the Southern Hotel are that it is the "oldest, longest operating hotel or lodging establishment in the United States west of the Mississippi." It is also claimed that the building itself is the "largest, oldest brick building in North America west of the Mississippi."

HOTEL SAINTE GENEVIEVE

In 1906 ground was broken for the construction of the Hotel Sainte Genevieve. Decades later, the Hotel can boast that it has NEVER been closed! It is now a hotel, restaurant, and lounge. It has remained open and inhabited through floods, and even during its restoration following a fire in the 1960s.

Some of the building's interior and some of the exterior walls are original, proving the strength in the life of the Hotel Sainte Genevieve.

SOUTHEAST REGION

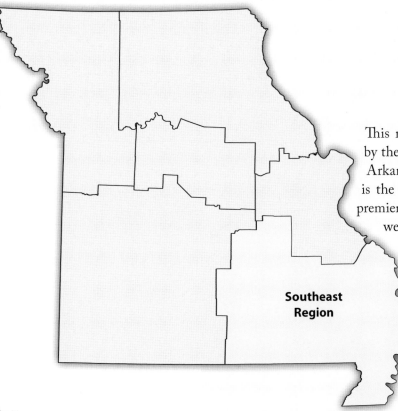

This region of Missouri is boarded on the east by the Mississippi River and on the south by the Arkansas State Line. In the northwest corner is the home of University of Missouri, Rolla, a premier mining and engineering university. The western edge of the area is defined by the Big Pitney River and in the southwest by Howell County and West Plains.

Numerous rivers cut through the region, making it a natural location for early pioneers to settle and build the many mills that dot the area.

Natural geological sites such as Elephant Rocks State Park, located in the Arcadia Valley near Ironton, attract rock hounds from far and wide.

The historical little town of Burfordville is home to the only site in the state of both a covered bridge and a mill.

An architectural look back in time is evident in the Port Cape Girardeau building, dating back to the early 1800s.

Jackson, Missouri boasts a real working tourist railroad in John's drawing of engine #5 and just down the road you can visit the Dillard Mill in Crawford County.

Near Eminence the beautiful Alley Spring Mill, depicted on the front cover of this book, sits near the Jacks Fork River and is operated by the National Park Service with mill tours in the summer.

Numerous state parks and historical sites abound in this region. The home of Southeast Missouri State University sits on the edge of the Mississippi River in Cape Girardeau, and not to be missed is the Mississippi River Observation Deck at New Madrid. Nearby is Sikeston, Missouri, home to Acclaim Press and the good folks who worked hard to make this book a reality.

BOLLINGER MILL AND BURFORDVILLE COVERED BRIDGE

Located on the outskirts of Burfordville, Missouri on Hwy. 34 west of Jackson, this grist mill represents a center of trade more than 150 years ago. Today's Bollinger Mill is actually the third one on the site. George Frederick Bollinger came to the Burfordville area in 1797. In his dealings for land, he agreed to bring more settlers from North Carolina, from where he came, and develop the land. In 1800, he returned with 20 families, including six of his brothers and their families.

They settled along the banks of the Whitewater River.

The 140-foot, self-supporting Howe Truss covered bridge sits adjacent to the mill, spanning the Whitewater River. The Civil War delayed the construction of the Burfordville Covered Bridge, but it was completed in 1868.

Both the Bollinger Mill and the Burfordville Covered Bridge are listed on the National Register of Historic Places, the bridge in 1970, and the mill in 1972.

DILLARD MILL

The Dillard Mill State Historic Site is one of Missouri's best preserved, water-powered grist mills. Much of the mill's equipment is still in place and actually operational. During tours of the mill, a simple turn of a wheel renders the machinery operational. Dillard Mill was completed in 1908, and as late as 1956, Dillard Mill still ground grain into flour and eventually into livestock feed.

Maintaining the feeling of days gone by, each Spring at Dillard Mill features an early 1900s picnic with music, old-time demonstrations, blacksmithing, and soap making among the many activities. Dillard Mill is located in Davisville in Crawford County.

THE MISSISSIPPI QUEEN

Oh my, close your eyes and drift back to Victorian days, then open your eyes and realize you're on the *Mississippi Queen*. This "boat" is the last of its kind… it runs totally on steam including its electrical system, the paddlewheel, and the world's largest calliope.

Geared mainly to the older generation, there is no babysitting service and no organized activities for children. Instead, the pace is slow and very relaxed. There is a movie theatre, but no casino, a small pool, and lots of scenery as you travel the "Mighty" Mississippi River. Quaint, small river cities in America's heartland are ports of call, i.e. Dubuque, Iowa, Hannibal, Missouri.

Families flock to their riverfronts to witness the breath-taking sight of the magnificent *Mississippi Queen* and the somewhat eerie sound of its calliope, leaving one feeling they've taken a step back in time.

Excursion Train, Engine #5

Jackson

"I think I can, I think I can…." Engine #5 knows it can, and it does! It does its job on diesel now rather than steam, but it takes you back to an era long gone.

The St. Louis Iron Mountain and Southern Railroad Corporation in 1851 was actually the first railroad company to build a railroad in Southeast Missouri. It was a working train, transporting iron ore from Iron Mountain, Missouri to the Mississippi River. Over the years, the railroad line was sold, finally being purchased by what is now Union Pacific.

Union Pacific deserted it in the mid-1980s and a development corporation purchased over 15 miles of track and right of way in order to keep railroad service open to Jackson.

A group of railway supporters organized and acquired a switch engine and several commuter cars. After great effort, time, labor, and tireless renovation, their tourist train was ready. Today, "Friends of Steam Railroading," a not-for-profit organization, provides financial support as well as volunteers for the St. Louis Iron Mountain and Southern Railway.

ELEPHANT ROCKS STATE PARK

During the Precambrian era about 1.5 billion years ago, molten rock, called magma, accumulated deep below the earth's surface. The magma slowly cooled, forming red granite rock that later weathered into huge, rounded boulders, looking like a herd of resting elephants, now the Elephant Rocks State Park.

No official count of the "elephants" inhabited in the Park has ever been taken, but one of the largest in the Park has affectionately been dubbed, "Dumbo." Dumbo weighs in at 680 tons.

There are many picnic sites in Elephant Rocks State Park, as well as two abandoned granite quarries. Stone that was quarried here is known commercially as Missouri red monument stone.

ALLEY SPRING MILL

Situated near Eminence, Missouri, Alley Spring Mill boasts a 100-year-old grist mill. Actually, the first mill was built in 1868, after which "a post office was established and named after a local farming family – Alley." The entire area became known as Alley, and the still-standing Alley Spring Mill was built 1893-1894. This mill was considered "high tech" for that period, using a turbine rather than a water wheel, and rollers instead of stone grist stones.

Alley Spring Mill was the hub of Alley and was vital to the community. Grain had to be ground to provide the daily bread. The mill was painted the infamous red color much later, and the color has become associated with Alley Spring Mill.

OLD APPLETON MILL

In 1824, Alfred McClain constructed his original mill on the north bank of Apple Creek in the old Spanish Cape Girardeau District. From 1824 to 1872, the mill operated as a grist mill, driven by a water wheel that turned French burrstones to grind corn meal and low quality flour. Additionally, the powder from the wheel was used to drive a sawmill that used a vertical blade in milling the lumber. In 1872, James McLane, then owner, replaced the water wheel with underwater turbines. Over time the mill had many owners and saw many changes until 1948 when it ceased production. In May of 1986, extremely high water washed the mill off its foundation and smashed it to pieces. John has created this drawing from old photography.

Southeast Missouri State University
Academic Hall

Southeast Missouri State University in Cape Girardeau has gone from Southeast Missouri State Normal School from 1873-1881, to what it is today, a public, accredited university. Likewise, the Old Normal Academic Building, Victorian in style, burned in an electrical fire in 1902. Standing today, having been built in 1906 using southeast Missouri limestone featured in its neoclassical design, Academic Hall is the hub of the Campus, housing all of the university's student services.

Standing with pride, Academic Hall is decorated with light fixtures from the 1904 St. Louis World's Fair. Keeping in mind that the Missouri state bird is the bluebird, the main floor of the hall is trimmed with mosaic tiles of bluebirds.

Port Cape Girardeau

Take a step back into the historic past of Cape Girardeau and dine in the beautifully restored and unique Port Cape Girardeau. Boasting as one of the "oldest standing structures west of the Mississippi River," dining at Port Cape Girardeau in its period décor is truly an event. The building is dated to circa 1830 to 1850. While dining, the Mississippi River just keeps on rollin' along, providing a spectacular view.

Although it's not included in John's drawing, a huge refurbished Coca-Cola sign is a signature part of the façade of the Port Cape Girardeau building.

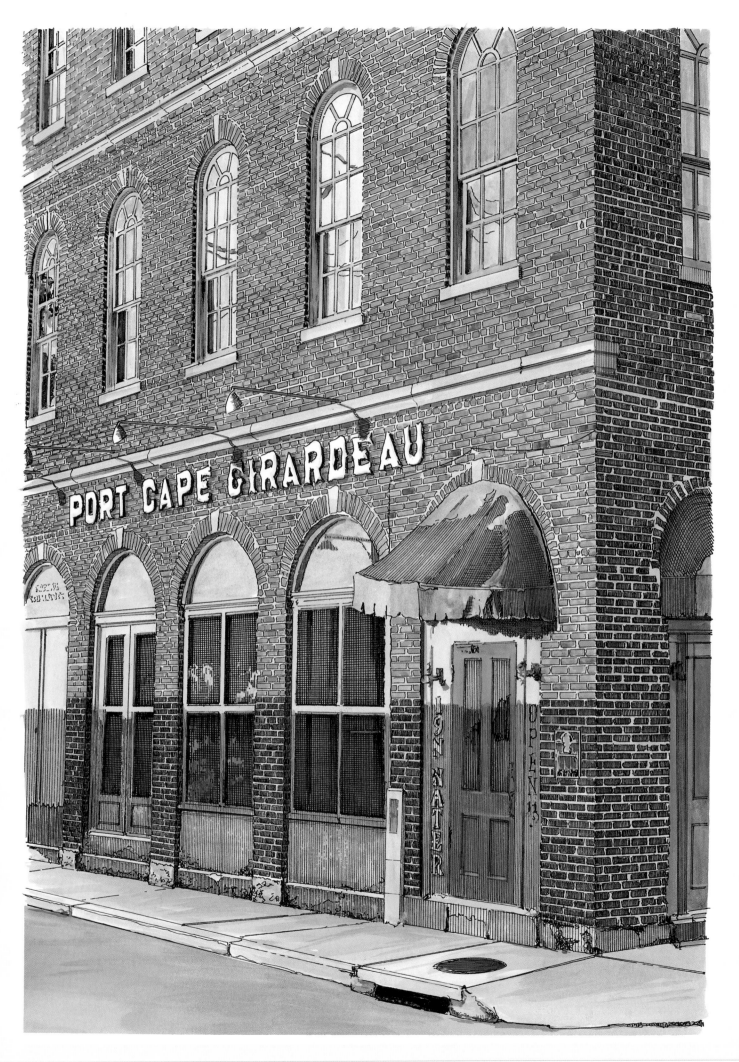

Northeast Region

The Reflections of Missouri Collection was born in the Northeast part of the state, specifically Hannibal, where John drew the Mark Twain Boyhood Home in the summer of 1991. From that drawing, he began to study the history of Missouri in his own "neck of the woods" and launched the creation of this entire collection of his artwork.

This section focuses on the area stretching from Moscow Mills in Lincoln County in the south, traveling north to the state line, including Kirksville and the campus at Truman State University and Culver Stockton College in Canton. Going west you'll find the Locust Creek Covered Bridge between Chillicothe and Brookfield.

On the east of this region is the Mississippi River and Louisiana, Missouri, home to John and his gallery and family. This area has been tagged "Little Dixie" due to the many Kentuckians and Virginians that settled in these "Golden Hills." The state's only scenic by-way is known as "The Little Dixie Highway" and it runs from south of Clarksville through Louisiana to just south of Hannibal. Running along the Mississippi River the drive is beautiful, with exquisite overlooks along the way and often entertainment from the winter eagle population.

Crossing the river at Louisiana is one of the oldest railroad bridges across the Mississippi River. Nearby in Bowling Green is the restored home of Speaker of the House, Champ Clark and north in Monroe County sits the Union Covered Bridge near Paris, Missouri.

South in Mexico, Missouri, one can visit the stately Missouri Military Academy built in 1889.

The region has much to offer visitors and historians alike, in a comfortable, rural setting.

Northeast
Region

BUCK BACKER BARN

The Backer barn is located in Pike County and is a designated "century barn," built out of native limestone.

MOSCOW MILLS

Can you imagine "travelling" from Kentucky to what we know today to be Moscow Mills in the early 1800s? Talk about "over the river and through the woods…." However, that is just what Christopher Clark did, and furthermore, he founded the first settlement at a spring that was later Wood's Fort in Troy. The Fort was erected after trouble with the Sac and Fox tribes.

One of the settlers, Shapley Ross, acquired a grist and saw mill on the Cuivre River near Christopher Clark's Fort. Using the native limestone, the home that Ross constructed still stands and is the home of the Lincoln Genealogical Society.

Moscow, as it was originally named, was platted a short distance from Clark's Fort. Moscow grew and in the 1830s the Old River Mill was constructed by Henry Martin. That Mill continued under various owners, operating until 1945, and is now the Mill Site Park.

In 1878, Moscow was renamed and according to some stores, "Mills" was added because of the grain mills that were constructed along the river.

SHAPLEY ROSS HOUSE
Circa 1820

The Shapley Ross House, located in Moscow Mills, is a two-story residence constructed of native limestone and a rare example of fine stonework masonry and Georgian-styled architecture. Originally restored by Mildred Depping and her sister, the late Irene Depping Langford, the house is currently owned by Charles and Laura Depping Meyer. It it listed on the National Register of Historic Places.

GRACE EPISCOPAL CHURCH

Clarksville

Clarksville, Missouri is such a lovely river town, with unique shops, friendly neighbors, and beautiful Missouri hills a part of the topography. Complimenting Clarksville's attributes is the lovely, historical Grace Episcopal Church. Grace Episcopal was the first Episcopal church in Clarksville, organized Palm Sunday, March 21, 1869.

The original frame building was torn down in 1940 and the new Grace Church was erected on the same site. The cornerstone was laid in November 1940. Dr. and Mrs. Malvern B. Clopton contributed financially, covering the entire cost of the new church.

Membership in Grace Episcopal has fluctuated over the years, beginning with its first 12 or so families. Recently, due in part to the lack of membership, Grace Episcopal no longer holds services and the Diocese of Missouri has decommissioned the church.

St. John's Episcopal Church

Prairieville (Eolia)

St. John's Episcopal Church is purported to be the oldest Episcopal church west of the Mississippi River, making it the oldest church in the Diocese of Missouri. Known as the "mother church" to Grace Episcopal in Clarksville and Calvary Episcopal in Louisiana, it has been host to weddings, funerals, and even sleeping quarters during the War Between the States as troops passed through the area. St. John's was completed in 1856 with a congregation made up principally of people from Virginia and Kentucky. A large part of the present members of St. John's are descendants of the early settlers who established the church, and it is they who keep the building in such exemplary condition, insuring the church for future generations to come.

On Sunday, October 11, 1956, Governor Lloyd Stark, native of Louisiana, Missouri, gave the address at St. John's centennial celebration. The wood-burning stoves on each side of the church provides the heat, and the same Bible given to St. John's by Peter Carr in 1856 rests on the same lectern as when the church was erected. St. John's Episcopal Church was placed on the National Register of Historic Places in 1970.

St. John's Episcopal Church is nestled in complete solitude of woods and the cemetery, and is a "monument to the faith in and love of the church."

LOUISIANA OVERVIEW

Louisiana, Missouri sits on the bank of the Mississippi River. Its Champ Clark Bridge crosses into Illinois and its railroad bridge is one of few still in use allowing trains to cross between Missouri and Illinois. Downtown Louisiana is listed on the National Register of Historic Places, its Missouri hills are known as Golden Hills, and its many artists create beautiful pieces of art, one of whom is John Stoeckley.

Louisiana has a cemetery covering one of its golden hills.

From its peak, one can see miles and miles of the Mississippi River and its banks, Missouri hills, rich farmland, and graves dating back to the Civil War. Riverview Cemetery is a part of the town that exemplifies the historical significance of Louisiana.

An overview of Louisiana is a "teaser." John's rendition actually is an invitation to check out what is on terra firma in Louisiana, Missouri.

CIVIL WAR MEMORIAL

Riverview Cemetery

Riverview Cemetery is located in Louisiana, Missouri. Shortly past the entrance to the Cemetery sits a Civil War Memorial constructed of "White Bronze" or zinc. A Union soldier stands watch and he represents the dedication "to all the brave defenders of the Union in 1861-1865, from the county of Pike, Missouri."

The Memorial was erected in 1884 by the Major James Wilson, Post #20 Grand Army of the Republic, Department of Missouri.

"On Fame's Eternal Camping Ground,
Their Silent Tents Are Spread,
And Glory Guards With Solemn Round,
The Bivouac Of Our Dead."

Louisiana Public Library

The Louisiana Public Library, built in 1904 in late Gothic Revival style architecture, is proudly listed on the National Register of Historic Places.

Between 1889-1929, Andrew Carnegie provided funding for the construction of over 1,600 libraries in the USA, and his philanthropy required the recipient town to share in funding with matching benefits. For instance, the Louisiana Public Library had a pledge of $10,000 from Andrew Carnegie and that amount to be matched by the citizens of Louisiana. More than 1,600 Carnegie libraries have been built in the United States. "When the last grant was made in 1919, there were 3,500 libraries in the United States, nearly half of them paid for by Carnegie." The Louisiana Public Library is among the first Carnegie libraries in the state of Missouri, as well as one of the first west of the Mississippi River.

LOUISIANA RAILROAD BRIDGE

The Louisiana Railroad Bridge depicted here by John was opened for service in 1873. The bridge boasts a single-track rail line crossing the beautiful Mississippi River from Pike County, Missouri to Pike County, Illinois. The bridge is a through truss swing railroad bridge with a total length of 2,053 feet, including a 446-foot swing-through truss. This truss opens allowing river traffic, such as the barge seen in this drawing, to pass. Certainly this bridge is one of the oldest, still-in-use swing bridges. It's quite a sight to see a train crossing the river via this long-standing bridge in Louisiana, Missouri.

STARK BEAR BARN

Louisiana

Stark Brothers Nurseries grew to be the "Largest in the World – Oldest in America." The famous botanist and horticulturist Luther Burbank made this possible when he told his wife that there really was only one organization in the world that was equipped to go forward with his work and make the most of his plant breeding. On his deathbed in 1926, he selected Stark Brothers Nurseries to carry on his work and willed over 750 varieties to the company. After his death, Mrs. Burbank followed through with his wishes and the rest is history, as they say!

The Stark Bear trademark has been featured for over 100 years in advertising, catalogs, signs on barns, and fruit shows all over America. The slogan "Stark Trees Bear Fruit" was created and the bear-shaped trademark followed. Wisely Stark Brothers Nurseries was one of the first to realize the value of advertising. They did so in weekly publications that circulated throughout America and abroad even as early as 1887.

The Stark Brothers Nurseries home office remains in Louisiana, Missouri. From that office, the Stark Bear with the words "Stark Trees Bear Fruit" can be seen on a nearby barn.

HONEY SHUCK

Home of James Beauchamp (Champ) Clark

This unimposing gingerbread home on a back street of Bowling Green, Missouri was the scene of many decisions that affected the course of United States history. Home to "Champ" Clark, the Speaker of the House from 1911 through the First World War to 1919, the house has been lovingly restored by friends of Honey Shuck. The home was named Honey Shuck because of the Honey Locust trees that once surrounded the house.

Champ Clark settled in Bowling Green in 1880, serving the next decade as City Attorney, Pike County Prosecuting Attorney and State Legislator. He was elected to the National House of Representatives in 1892, and remained in the House until 1920. A few months after his defeat in 1920, he died and is buried in Bowling Green.

In 1912, at the Baltimore Democratic Convention, Champ received 440 ½ votes on the first ballot to the 324 votes for Woodrow Wilson. He continued to lead the field until the 14th ballot. Prior to the convention, he campaigned in several Midwest states for the Grass Roots, traditional American vote. His theme song was "Don't Kick My Dawg Around."

Union Covered Bridge

The Union Covered Bridge, near Paris, Missouri, has the honor of claiming to be the *only* "Burr-arch" covered bridge left in Missouri. The bridge was built by Joseph C. Elliot in 1871, using the Burr-arch truss system.

Mr. Theodore Burr, after whom the "Burr-arch Truss" design became known, used two long arches resting on the abutments on either end, that typically sandwiched a multiple kingpost structure. Mr. Burr patented his new truss system in 1804.

The Union Bridge was built in 1871 and was named for the Union Church, which once stood nearby the 125 foot-long bridge. It was placed on the National Register of Historic Places in 1970.

Ralls County Courthouse

New London

The first Ralls County Courthouse was completed in 1822, but the third and still-standing courthouse was completed in 1858. Not only is it still standing, it is considered the most beautiful courthouse in Missouri. Today, the Ralls County Courthouse is listed on the National Register of Historic Places.

MEADOWCREST

This snowy scene depicts winters in Northeast Missouri at the home of John and Karen Stoeckley in the country.

HANNIBAL'S MAIN STREET

This peek down the Main Street of Hannibal, Missouri looks very much as it did during the young days of Samuel Clemens. Shops and restaurants and cafes dot the scene and welcome thousands of annual visitors.

MARK TWAIN
Samuel Langhorne Clemens, 1835-1910

Mark Twain is the most read American author throughout the world. His genius was not only for humor and adventure, he was also known for his great humanity and vision. His most popular works: *The Adventures of Tom Sawyer*, 1876; *The Adventures of Huckleberry Finn*, 1884; *The Prince and the Pauper*, 1881; *Pudd'nhead Wilson*, 1894; *The Celebrated Jumping Frog of Calaveras County*, 1865; *The Connecticut Yankee at King Arthur's Court*, 1889; have been translated into nearly every foreign language and remain popular more than 100 years after they were first published.

The spirit of Mark Twain lives on in his boyhood home, Hannibal, Missouri (shown on page 105).

Mark Twain Lighthouse

On Cardiff Hill in Hannibal, Missouri, a lighthouse was erected to celebrate the 100th Anniversary of Mark Twain's birth. The Lighthouse was never intended to aid navigation, "but to shine light over the year-long festivities surrounding the celebration of Mark Twain's birthday." It is the only lighthouse built inland, and it features a panoramic view of both Hannibal and the Mississippi River.

In 1935, President Franklin D. Roosevelt turned the Lighthouse beam on for the first time by pressing a gold key that was connected to telegraph lines, making it possible all the way from the nation's capital. In 1963, when the beacon was rededicated, President John F. Kennedy also had the privilege, as did President Bill Clinton in 1994.

TOM SAWYER, BECKY THATCHER AND HUCK FINN

The famous fence of Tom Sawyer gets white-washed by Huckleberry Finn as Tom's first love looks on at this amazing turn of events. Tom has convinced Huck that engaging in this activity is truly a great opportunity for Huck. How Tom managed to get Huck to do Tom's work is part of the wonderful tales written by Mark Twain. Today, this famous fence can be seen next to the boyhood home of Mark Twain in Hannibal, Missouri. The fence painting scene is reenacted each summer and a new Tom and Becky are selected to represent these colorful characters in the famous tales, *The Adventures of Tom Sawyer and Huckleberry Finn.*

MARK TWAIN'S BOYHOOD HOME

The adventures of Tom Sawyer, Huckleberry Finn and Becky Thatcher live on today in Hannibal, Missouri, virtually unchanged since the days of young Samuel Clemens. Hannibal is proud of its hero and does everything imaginable to keep Twain's memory alive, including maintaining this boyhood home of Samuel Clemens and providing daily tours.

TOM AND HUCK

After passing the Mark Twain Boyhood Home in the town of Hannibal, Mr. George Mahan commissioned sculptor Frederick Hibbard to create a statue of Mark Twain's two best known characters, Tom Sawyer and Huck Finn.

The statue was dedicated on May 27, 1926 at ceremonies at the foot of Cardiff Hill. Mr. Hibbard created the statue to depict that moment in Tom's life when he awoke to the world and wanted to go out and see it for himself. Hence the knapsack, the advanced foot and the whole posture of his body.

American Queen Riverboat

"Old Man River, that Old Man River...." Board the *American Queen* riverboat and you'll think you're on Broadway in "Show Boat" as it travels the Old South and the Heartland of America. The *American Queen* has been said to be a "floating Victorian palace." Shall we sip a mint julep or lemonade on the "front porch" in a rocking chair, or maybe choose one of its six decks on which to relax?

The *American Queen* boasts being the world's largest steamboat, as well as the world's largest river cruise ship. Her pilothouse and stacks are designed to be lowered, which makes it possible for her to pass under bridges. Yes, the *American Queen* riverboat is the crème de la crème of river cruising.

Hannibal-LaGrange University

In 1858, LaGrange College was founded in LaGrange, Missouri. In 1928, LaGrange College moved to Hannibal, Missouri, and the school was renamed Hannibal-LaGrange College. The citizens of Hannibal wanted a Baptist college, and they made sufficient financial pledges to make their dream a reality; thus, the merging of LaGrange College and Hannibal-LaGrange College and the relocation to Hannibal. LaGrange College brought with it the Baptist association, and Hannibal had the financial ability to provide a beautiful new campus. In 2010, this educational institution became a university.

Culver-Stockton College
Canton

Culver-Stockton College was founded as Christian University in 1853, in Canton, Missouri.

The college was renamed following the Civil War, after Mary Culver and Robert Stockton, both from St. Louis, donated generously toward the rebuilding of the school. During the Civil War, troops occupied the school's only building, Old Main. The building was left in terrible condition, and contents destroyed, as was the "campus." Mary Culver's husband, Lucius Llewellyn Culver, and Robert Stockton became business partners, and later generous donors to the college.

Missouri Military Academy

Mexico

Missouri Military Academy, Mexico, Missouri, was founded in 1889, and fire destroyed the academy in 1896. The rebuilt school was at a new site and its doors opened once more in 1900.

Very active in the rebuilding of the academy, among many others of course, was Colonel C.R. Stribling Jr. Stribling had been on the faculty for 13 years, and in 1933 he took command of the academy. It was under his command that the "Academy solidified its position as one of the nation's leading prep schools." In 1968, Colonel Stribling's son, Colonel Charles R. Stribling III, served as president of the school for 25 years. The administration building was renamed in 1981 in honor of Colonel Stribling.

Missouri Military Academy celebrated its Centennial in 1989, four years after being named one of the nation's Exemplary Private Schools by the U.S. Department of Education. Young men in grades 6-12 are accepted at the academy.

MACON COUNTY COURTHOUSE
Macon

The Macon County Courthouse was originally built in Bloomington, Missouri, in 1838. In 1863, an act of legislature moved the site to Macon City. Because of citizen's pro Southern leanings, orders were to burn the entire town of Bloomington. Through some political moves, a bill was presented to move the Macon County Seat from Bloomington to Macon.

The Macon County Courthouse is on the National Register of Historic Places. The building was erected in 1865 and still stands today. The style is "Romanesque Revival," featuring round arches and thick, massive walls, with typical Italian detailing.

MACON (BLEES) MILITARY ACADEMY

Colonel Frederick Wm. V. Blees inherited interests in Germany and used that wealth to build what he hoped would be his legacy, the construction of the Blees Military Academy in Macon. The academy offered the Blees cadets every luxury, accommodation and opportunity.

The Academic Hall was originally built to be fireproof, therefore little wood was used on the interior or the exterior. The gymnasium was the other major building, housing an indoor running track, a swimming pool, showers, and other rooms.

Unfortunately, Blees died in 1906 and the academy went bankrupt. The buildings remained unoccupied until 1915 when Dr. Arthur G. Hildreth and Charles E. and Harry M. Still, sons of Andrew Taylor Still, the founder of the profession of osteopathic medicine, established a sanatorium.

The Academic Hall and Gymnasium are now on the National Register of Historic Places and are used for low income housing for citizens of Macon.

LOCUST CREEK
COVERED BRIDGE

The Locust Creek Covered Bridge originally played an important part in northern Missouri, in that it provided passage over Locust Creek and a connection on America's first transcontinental road, Route 8. However, in 1930, U.S. Highway 36 replaced Route 8, leaving the Locust Creek Covered Bridge "off the beaten track."

In addition to the lack of traffic, the Locust Creek's channel was redirected and the bridge ended up resting on solid ground due to filling, blowing topsoil, and other weather elements.

The Locust Creek Covered Bridge was later repaired and preserved by the Missouri Park Board. After its restoration, the bridge was placed on the National Register of Historic Places. At that time it was raised six feet to give it once again the appearance of a bridge. The bridge is located in Linn County, Missouri.

KIRKSVILLE COLLEGE OF OSTEOPATHIC AND SURGERY

Andrew Taylor Still founded the American School of Osteopathy in 1892. His school combined with another, names were changed, and then in 1926, Kirksville College of Osteopathy and Surgery emerged.

Andrew Taylor Still was born in 1828 in Lee County, Virginia. His father was a physician. Andrew studied and apprenticed as a physician with his father. He actually earned a formal M.D. degree in Baldwin, Kansas.

Having seen the dread of medicine and medical treatment during the Civil War, and having lost three of his children to spinal meningitis and one from pneumonia, Andrew became disenchanted with medicines as they were at that time. He began seeking alternative methods of healing, which ultimately led him to the philosophy "that all body systems are interrelated and dependent upon one another for good health."

Andrew Taylor Still, M.D., D.O., is known as the "father of osteopathic medicine" and was the founder of the first college of osteopathic medicine.

TRUMAN STATE UNIVERSITY
Kirksville

Truman State University can be remembered as Northeast Missouri State University, 1972; Northeast Missouri State University, 1967; Northeast Missouri State College, 1919; Northeast Missouri State Teachers College; and in the beginning September 2, 1867, North Missouri Normal School and Commercial College. Today, Truman State University offers a wide span of degrees offered by a liberal arts institution for undergraduate education.

Originally established primarily to prepare teachers for public schools, later expanding and becoming designated as Truman State University, the school became recognized as Missouri's only statewide public liberal arts and sciences university.

When Northeast Missouri State University became Truman State University, it was named in honor of the only Missourian to become President of the United States, Harry S Truman.

CENTRAL REGION

The central part of Missouri is defined in this book by Callaway County and Osage County on the East. To the west are Saline and Pettis counties and Howard County in the north, with the towns of Fayette and Glasgow creating an imaginary boundary that John has used to capture the region. Cole County on the south is home to the Missouri State Capitol in Jefferson City. Follow the Missouri River as it boarders the northwest and turns south at Glasgow, sweeping down past Boonville in the center, then dipping down to Jefferson City from the West.

Just north of the capitol is the renowned University of Missouri, Columbia, the original land grant college of the state, and today a major player in the field of higher education in the nation. John has captured numerous sites on campus; his first being Jesse Hall, drawn on site when his son, Denton, attended school there in the early 90s. The drawing of the columns has been a favorite with many graduates and the old joke that John often asks graduates – "did you know that two of the columns are farther apart than the others?" – brings many a laugh to the situation when he points to the two end columns!

Farther west, a 1909 circa castle having its own state park is the Bothwell Lodge, which looms high on the bluffs near Sedalia.

The central part of the state is home to numerous wineries, not the least of which is Les Bourgeois, sitting high above the north east side of the Missouri River, with its bountiful vineyards in the surrounding areas. John and Karen own The Eagle's Nest Winery in Louisiana, Missouri and have their wines made at the Les Bourgeois location by master wine maker Cory Boomgras. A trip through the central portion of the state calls for visits to some of the many wineries in this area.

A visit to Fulton, Missouri reveals the international history of World War II at the Churchill memorial on the campus of Westminster University. John has captured the history and times of a number of sites in Fulton, including William Woods' campus landmarks.

Central Region

STATE CAPITOL
Jefferson City

The original Capitol building in Jefferson City burned in 1837, and the Missouri Governor's Mansion is presently on that site. The current building was completed in 1840, and this structure also burned on February 5, 1911 when it was struck by lightning.

Sixty-nine architecture firms submitted designs, and Tracy & Swarthout from New York was selected. The Missouri State Capitol is noted for its architectural features, which include eight 48-foot columns on the south, and six 40-foot columns on the north, a 30-foot-wide stairway, and 13 by 18 feet bronze front doors – "the largest cast since the Roman era." The stone for the exterior is a dense marble from Carthage, Missouri.

The Capitol's dome rises 238 feet above ground level and is topped by the goddess of vegetation, Ceres, symbolizing Missouri's strength in agriculture.

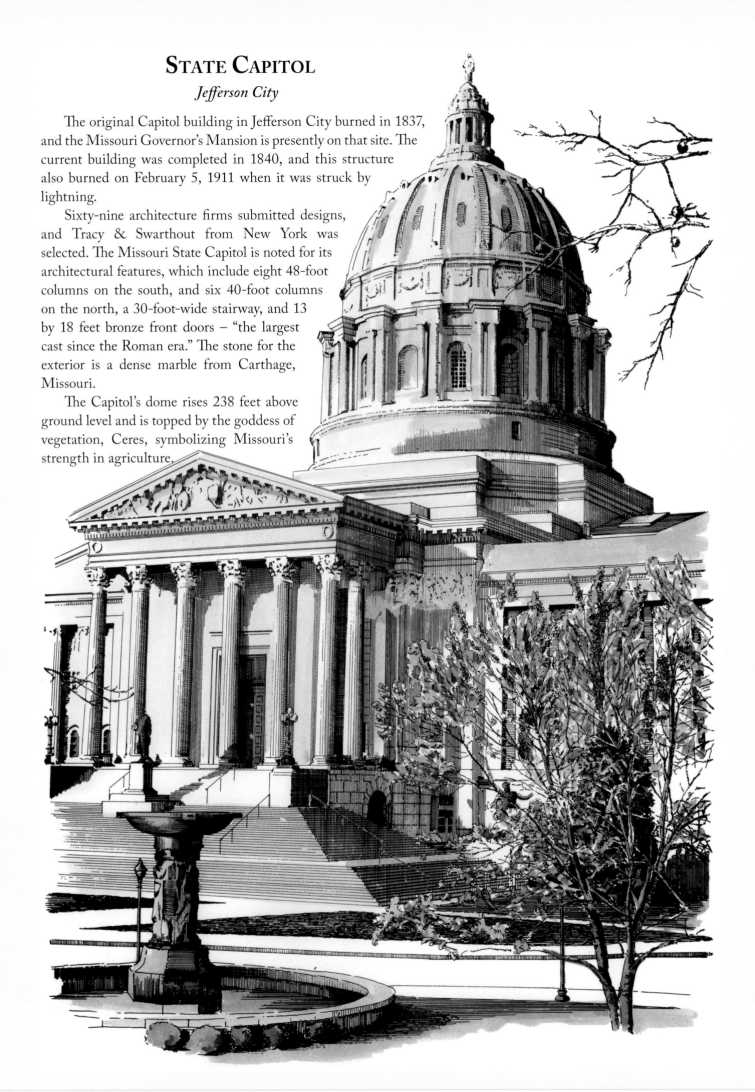

LOHMAN'S LANDING

Jefferson City

In 1826, James A. Crump built a sturdy stone structure that became known as the Lohman Building. The area around the Lohman Building grew with a grocery store, warehouse, tavern, telegraph office and hotel, and the area became known as the Landing.

The state later acquired the Lohman Building, which boasts being the oldest existing building in Jefferson City. It was to be destroyed, but was met with great strength to preserve the building. The Lohman Building was saved and placed on the National Register of Historic Places in 1969. The building is now open to the public as the cornerstone of Jefferson Landing State Historic Site. Exhibits on the history of the capital city are housed in the Lohman Building, and it also is a support facility for the Missouri State Museum, which is located in the State Capitol.

Supreme Court

In 1907, the Supreme Court Building in Jefferson City became a permanent home for the court. The building was constructed using funds that were raised by the World's Fair in 1904.

Because the building was constructed before there was indoor lighting, the library, which is on the second level, has glass floors, allowing light from the windows to filter down to the main floor. This library houses over 110,000 volumes, and welcomes those searching for resources.

WINSTON CHURCHILL AND THE BERLIN WALL

Winston Churchill delivered his "Sinews of Peace" address at Westminster College in Fulton, Missouri, on March 5, 1946. In this address, he stated that, "an iron curtain has descended across the continent." This address became popularly known as the "Iron Curtain" speech.

Churchill came to Fulton at the urging of President Harry Truman who did, in fact, introduce Churchill prior to his delivery of the address. Winston Churchill was a master orator, with the ability to command attention and hold an audience in his hand.

Very appropriately Winston Churchill's granddaughter, Edwina Sandys, introduced her sculpture "Breakthrough" one year after the fall of the Berlin Wall. "Breakthrough" is made from eight sections of the Berlin Wall. The sculpture both memorializes Churchill's "Sinews of Peace" address, but also commemorates the fall of the Berlin Wall.

WESTMINSTER COLLEGE
THE COLUMNS
Fulton

The Columns, located on The Hill, are the only remnant of the original Westminster Hall, destroyed by fire in 1909. Two of the most revered Westminster traditions are the Fall Convocation, when new students enter the campus through The Columns, and Commencement, when graduating students pass back through The Columns into the world.

JOE'S PUMPKIN PATCH

Shortly after moving to Louisiana, Missouri, John developed a special friendship with a fellow employee at Stark Bros. Nurseries, Joe Preczewski. Later, Joe moved his family to Marthasville, Missouri, and established a fruit orchard on one of the rolling hillsides. In a valley area below the house and orchard, Joe planted pumpkins for sale to the St. Louis grocery stores. The Stoeckley family would join Joe's family for pumpkin picking and family dinners. When Joe was diagnosed with cancer, John created this picture for Joe and his family. Today, the picture reminds us of those wonderful family times together and Joe's strong work ethic, and how fortunate the Stoeckley family was to have had this special friendship.

TWO PAINTED PONIES — MAMA AND BABY

While traveling the state of Missouri, some uniquely beautiful things would catch the artist's eye. What is more tender than a mother and her child... whether it be human or animal! Thus is the case here...

KEMPER MILITARY SCHOOL

Boonville

Kemper opened in 1844 as the Boonville Boarding School," an all-male school. Frederick T. Kemper operated the school basically by himself, and he freely and often changed the name of the school, including Male Collegiate Institute, Kemper Family School, and others. Kemper was one of few schools to continue operating during the Civil War. The school wisely remained neutral during the war.

Kemper officially changed its name to Kemper Military School in 1899, and began to advertise itself as "The West Point of the West." It was during this time that Will Rogers attended the school, certainly one of the more prominent alumni.

Kemper Military School's campus and facilities are now owned by the City of Boonville and known as Frederick T. Kemper Park. The school functioned on many different levels from June 3, 1844 to June 3, 2002.

KATY DEPOT

Boonville

The Boonville station is the only surviving Spanish Mission-style depot on the Missouri, Kansas, Texas Railroad (Katy Railroad). At its peak, 25 to 30 trains came through Boonville per day. However, the automobile and the completion of Interstate 70 marked the end of an era. The last passenger trains through Boonville were in 1958, after which the Katy Railroad closed the depot. The last freight trains through were in 1986, marking the closing of the Katy Railroad. After restoration and preservation of the Boonville Katy Depot in 1995, it is now the home of the Boonville Area Chamber of Commerce and Tourist Information Center and District offices of the Division of State Parks.

ROSLYN HEIGHTS

Boonville

Constructed in 1895 for Wilbur T. and Rhoda Stephens Johnson as their private residence, the house is of Queen Anne style architecture and Romanesque Revival affinities, housing 18 rooms and a spring floor ballroom on the third floor. The Johnsons named their home "Roslyn Heights." Located at 821 Main Street, it is considered the "last of the Main Street mansions" of Boonville in Cooper County.

Today, the Missouri State Society Daughters of the American Revolution own the home and were instrumental in having Roslyn Heights placed on the National Register of Historical Places in 1990. The organization has the house open April through December with a Christmas Open House the first week of December.

THESPIAN HALL

Boonville

Thespian Hall in Boonville is under the protection of The National Register of Historic Places, and is home for the Boonville Community Theater and is also used for other community events.

Thespian Hall was built in 1857, the first floor a theater, second floor a meeting place for the Masonic and Odd Fellow lodges and City Hall, and the basement a library and reading room. The Thespian Society, organized in 1838, demonstrated the early interest in cultural activities. Proceeds from the Society's performances were used for the erection of Thespian Hall.

Linn Memorial Methodist Church

Paul H. Linn Memorial Methodist Church, located on the campus of Central Methodist College in Fayette, was consecrated in June of 1930. Dr. Linn, for whom the church was named, was president of the college from July 1913 to February 1924. Cross Memorial Tower, behind the church, displays the clock which was in the Centenary Chapel, the structure originally on the site.

Howard County Courthouse

Fayette

The first Howard County Courthouse was constructed in 1826, with the interior completed in 1827 and one year later the building itself was completed (including 30 pairs of window shutters).

In 1857, Joseph Megraw built Howard County's second courthouse. He was given a budget of $25,000 for the two-story brick building. He added some special touches, including a cupola with a clock, weathervane, and an eagle decorating the front. Fire destroyed the building in 1886.

In 1887, an architectural firm of Kansas City was employed to create the plans, drawings and specifications for Howard County's third courthouse. On December 31, 1975, the building was gutted by fire. The exterior walls of the building withstood the fire, but the entire interior was destroyed.

Now on the Fayette Courthouse Square Historic District, Fayette remains the county seat housed in the county's fourth courthouse.

GLASGOW RAILROAD BRIDGE

The Glasgow Railroad Bridge was built in 1878 and 1879. It was the world's first all-steel bridge. It was the decision of the chief engineer, General Sooy Smith, to use new "alloys of iron and steel" developed by an Iowa gentleman, A. T. Hay.

There were skeptics of the new steel, of course, and sure enough during the construction one of the steel spans gave way. It was concluded that it was not due to the lack of strength of the steel, rather the span was bent, but the steel showed "no fracture in the material." This happening proved the strength of the steel and the Glasgow Railroad Bridge was completed on June 7, 1879.

Over the years, railroads developed faster locomotives and weights were increasing. By 1899, the need for a new bridge became vital and was constructed in 1900 using some of the substructure of the original bridge.

OUR LADY HELP OF CHRISTIANS

Frankenstein

Originally Our Lady Help of Christians Church was organized in 1863, and after three different locations in its first 27 years, the present church was dedicated on September 1, 1923. German and Irish immigrants settled in Frankenstein where the parish was started.

The exterior of the church and the bell tower are quarried native limestone and the design is Romanesque. The roof is of red Italian tile. The dedicated Parishioners donated most of the labor and the Church stands today as a living memorial to the priests and people of Frankenstein who built it with love and sacrifice as a gift to God.

Our Lady Help of Christians is, of course, a small, rural parish. It has kept a family image. Parishioners assume responsibility for the ministry and upkeep of the parish property.

MISSOURI VALLEY COLLEGE
Marshall

Baity Hall on the Missouri Valley College campus stands in tact today as it did when it was built in 1888-1889, of course, with some conservation and restoration. Baity Hall, known as "Old Main" until 1948, when it was renamed for Reverend George P. Baity, stood as the only building on the Missouri Valley College campus. It had classrooms, offices, a chapel, a museum, and a gymnasium for both men and women. It was "the home for many prospective ministers for the Missouri and Kansas synods of the Cumberland Presbyterian Church, which founded the school." With great pride, Baity Hall is listed on the National Register of Historic Places.

LYCEUM THEATRE

Arrow Rock

In 1960, the Arrow Rock Baptist Church building was sold and the Arrow Rock Lyceum Theatre was established.

Every summer, the Lyceum Theatre is full to overflow with people who come to the 408-seat theatre to see the high caliber plays directed by professional directors and performed by professional actors. These professionals, along with professional designers and technicians, reside in Arrow Rock for the duration of the "season."

Arrow Rock has earned many historic honors, among them, having been designated a National Historic Landmark by the Department of the Interior, National Park Service. In 1964, the entire town of Arrow Rock was designated a National Historic Landmark.

J. Huston Tavern

Arrow Rock

Virginian Joseph Huston settled in Arrow Rock in 1819. In 1833 he purchased block 17 in the town and began construction of a two-and-one-half story Federal-style building. By 1840, the building was widely known as a hotel and as business increased from travelers, Huston built an addition to the structure that housed a mercantile shop. Between 1850 and 1870, a frame addition was constructed housing a dining room and tavern. It is purported that the tavern has continuously served meals since the Civil War. It is now managed by the Missouri Department of Natural Resources, serving family-style, country meals.

UNIVERSITY OF MISSOURI, COLUMBIA

Jesse Hall, Alumni Center, Tiger Plaza

This collage represents various scenes and buildings located on the campus of the University of Missouri, Columbia. The 1,200-pound bronze tiger statue sits amid the Tiger Plaza fountain, a gift from the alumni association, near the Donald W. Reynolds Alumni Center.

Academic Hall was originally built in 1892 and subsequently burned, with its replacement built in 1895 and 27 years later renamed in honor of the university president, retiring Richard Henry Jesse. Jesse Hall boasts a majestic nine-story high dome, which was first lighted in 1987 to celebrate Missouri University's sesquicentennial.

THE COLUMNS

On January 9, 1892, a Saturday night, a crowd was assembling in the chapel for a performance of the Athenian Literary Society of the University of Missouri, Columbia, when faulty wiring ignited a fire in the ceiling and caused the central chandelier to come down. Academic Hall was ablaze. Today, the columns are all that remain of that building; they have become the focal point of the campus.

STEPHENS COLLEGE
Senior Hall

Stephens College is located in Columbia, Missouri and Senior Hall is the oldest building on campus for this all-girls college. There is a tale involving Senior Hall that dates back to October 31st, Halloween night, just after the close of the Civil War.

June Wheeler lived in Senior Hall during the Civil War. From this point on, there are many variations of the "story," – pick one. Sarah was late getting to dinner one night and she heard knocking at her door. It so happened that it was Issac Johnson,

a Confederate soldier, possible/probable rebel, all battered and torn. Sarah hid him in the Bell Tower, tended his wounds, and brought food to him taken from the dining hall. Chapter Two: They fell in love! Chapter Three: While attempting to escape together, they drowned in the swollen Missouri River (actually the Hinkson Creek is more feasible), nevertheless romantically and together they drowned! Many versions of this "tale" are told, but on Halloween the seniors attending Stephens College enjoy the tradition of the lovers revisiting Senior Hall.

COLUMBIA COLLEGE GATES

Rogers Gates lead you into the main campus of Columbia College in Columbia. When the college received its charter from the Missouri Legislature in 1851, it was Christian College. Christian College was the first women's college west of the Mississippi River to be charted by a state legislature. It has always had an affiliation "by covenant" with the Christian Church (Disciples of Christ), but also has always been nonsectarian.

Moving ahead to the 1960s, Christian College was not the only small private college to face problems with declining enrollments, but Christian College faced the times head on and made necessary changes to stay afloat. In 1970, Christian College changed from a two-year all-female college to a four-year coeducational college and also changed its name to Columbia College.

ROCHEPORT TUNNEL

In Rocheport, you either walk or ride a bicycle through the Rocheport Tunnel. This tunnel was built in 1893 for the Missouri-Kansas-Texas Railroad, nicknamed "Katy." You don't have to walk the railroad tracks to get through the tunnel, as the tracks were removed when the railroad right-of-way and the tunnel were converted to the Katy Trail.

The nostalgic Rocheport Tunnel is partial brick lined, partial stone and mortar lined and partial natural. There is no question that it was definitely built to last. It withstood the many trains going through it, and now bicyclists and walkers enjoy the Rocheport Tunnel.

SEDALIA DEPOT

aka Katy Depot

It's 1958, the Missouri-Kansas-Texas (Katy) passenger train just left Sedalia, 88 years after the first MKT train went from Sedalia to Clinton. This was the last passenger train to pass through.

The Katy Depot opened in 1896. Due to the foresight of the architect, Bradford L. Gilbert, the Sedalia Depot was built with materials that would resist flying sparks from diesel engines. Stone and brick were used rather than wood,

and central heating instead of stoves – these less hazardous materials have served the Sedalia Depot well.

Sedalia's Katy Depot is a splendid structure reminiscent of the railroad "era." In its prime, it housed a three-sided ticket office, an open passenger pavilion, a women's waiting room, a men's waiting room, a baggage room, and the dining hall that was considered Sedalia's finest eating establishment when the Depot opened.

Old Sedalia Bridge

There is just something nostalgic about old covered bridges. The covered bridge just outside Sedalia, Missouri conjures up such sentiment. In 1881, John Cornelius Johnnesen (remembered as John C. Johnson) was chartered to design a covered bridge to cross the Flat Creek. This immediately gave Sedalia year-round crossing, thus enhancing "commercial and pedestrian traffic to other townships south of Sedalia." Johnson was paid twenty-five dollars for his design of the covered bridge.

So the stories go, the covered bridge became almost park-like, with picnickers, swimmers and sweethearts strolling across the bridge, and a favorite fishing spot. For 85 years the bridge stood proudly and useful until 1966, when it burned to the ground. It has always been speculated that it was vandalism, but never proven. Nevertheless, the covered bridge is gone!

However, thanks to many for both funding and volunteer efforts, a new "old" covered bridge, scale replica, stands in Sedalia's Centennial Park.

Bothwell Lodge
Sedalia

Known as Sedalia's Castle on the Hill, this intriguing mansion took thirty-one years and four building phases to complete. It was built between 1897 and 1928 by John Homer Bothwell from Maysville, Illinois. He had moved to Sedalia in 1871 and began his practice as an attorney in town.

The 12,000-square-foot lodge was a recreational retreat for Bothwell and his many guests. There are thirty-one rooms on three floors, plus the tower. It is built over three caves, of which one is below a stairwell that has openings to the various floors, drawing the cool air to the rooms above the caves. Native rock from the property was used to build the four sections of the lodge.

As a good promoter and supporter of Sedalia, he was president of the Sedalia Board of Trade and the Sedalia National Bank as well as serving as an assistant prosecuting attorney. He represented the Sedalia area for eight years as a legislator to the Missouri General Assembly and unsuccessfully ran for governor in 1904. His influence helped to make Sedalia the permanent location for the Missouri State Fair.

Mr. Bothwell gifted the lodge and the surrounding area to the state and it is now operated as a state historical site, demonstrating the fascinating architectural design, fixtures and furnishings of the 1800s. The surrounding area is called Stonyridge Trails, and is available for hiking and sightseeing from the beautiful view above the plain.

From Springfield, Missouri's third largest city to the shores of Lake Taneycomo, wonderful opportunities are around every bend of the road, from excellent institutions of higher learning to the best trout fishing in the state to live entertainment in the many show places in Branson. This area of Missouri offers something for everyone, young and old alike. History comes alive in Silver Dollar City with demonstrating craftsmen, over 40 daily shows and the Culinary & Craft School.

Rafting and water sports are unlimited from Table Rock Lake, Bull Shoals Lake, Stockton Lake for sailing, and the Elk River for floating. The Land of Lakes offers visitors and residents many enjoyable ways to vacation and visit educational and historical sites. Old water mills, courthouses, castle ruins, and a Sports Hall of Fame are just a few more interesting sites available.

LAKES REGION

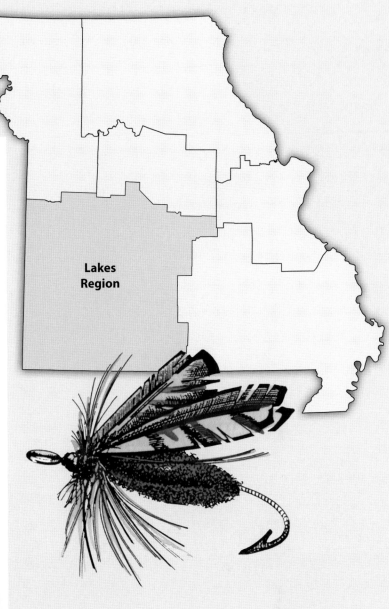

BENNETT SPRING

Originally Bennett Spring was named Brice Spring after the James Brice family who had settled there and built a mill on the site. Nearby, the Bennett family also built a mill. When the families were united by marriage, the spring became known as Bennett Spring.

Around 1900, the spring was stocked with mountain trout. A few years later a private fish hatchery was built at one of the old mill sites. After the area grew and became a focal point for fishermen, the Missouri State Park Board established Bennett Spring State Park, one of the first Missouri State parks.

Today, Bennett Spring is a favorite with fly fishermen and they flock there on opening day of trout season. Many of these same fishermen own this very piece of artwork in limited edition, given to them by wives, sweethearts and children for various occasions.

HA HA TONKA

The stark, vertical stone ruins of Ha Ha Tonka castle are all that remain of Robert McClure Snyder's dream. This private retreat included the European style 60-room castle, a stone carriage house, an 80-foot high water tower, and greenhouses. In 1942, sparks from a fireplace kindled a tragic fire that gutted the castle and the carriage house.

Today, the ruins and the property belong to the Missouri Department of Natural Resources, having opened the Ha Ha Tonka State Park in 1979. The state park is known for its complex of geologic features and formations, not the least of which are the 250-foot bluffs created by the collapse of ancient caves.

THE PONY

Missouri is known for fine horse stock and this drawing depicts
one of the quarterhorses favored by Missouri horsemen.

JAKE, THE MULE

Jake is a Missouri mule, which is the official state animal. The mule became the Missouri state animal in 1995 when then Governor, Mel Carnahan, signed a bill designating it so.

In addition to the mule's part in farming, Missouri mules pulled pioneer wagons, and were invaluable in transporting troops and supplies during World War I and II. The Show-Me State is proud to claim the mule as its official state animal.

OLD BARN AND OLD TREE

This scene is often repeated throughout the Missouri countryside, as farmers leave the country for the cities and commercial employment.

However, these scenes provide good studies for many Missouri artists, capturing a hint of the past before it has completely disappeared.

DAWT MILL

Built in 1887 by Alva Hodgson, this mill continues to serve as a center of activity for the area around Tecumseh, Missouri and the North Fork River nearby. This historic roller mill, which ground corn into meal for the families that journeyed there over 100 years ago, created the small village of Dawt that became a bustling community. At the turn of the century, in addition to the mill, store and post office, the property featured a blacksmith shop, sawmill, cotton gin, houses and a church. These businesses sprang up as a result of necessity. Farmers bringing their grain for milling conducted their business in Dawt as they waited their turn for the mill.

Hodgson Mill

Situated near Gainesville, Missouri, deep in the Missouri Ozarks, sits the Hodgson Mill. Mr. Alva Hodgson would be proud that his millwright abilities continue to live through the roots and history of his mill. The Hodgson Mill was being used by 1837; a second mill was built in 1861. That mill suffered destruction during the Civil War. In 1882, a paddle wheel mill was built and stands today as the Hodgson Mill.

Alva and his brother George took the mill's operation to a higher level, becoming one of the area's most profitable and well-known, continuing to thrive even into the early 1900s. Today, the mill is not only a tourist attraction, but it continues to stone grind grains. In 1969, the still-producing mill became officially known as Hodgson Mill and a similar drawing appears on the packages and bags of flour and meals sold.

WILDERNESS CHURCH
Silver Dollar City

Tucked away in a most secluded and beautiful setting in Silver Dollar City since 1849 is the Wilderness Church. Today, Wilderness Church is available for private weddings.

The pulpit used in the chapel was hand-carved from a tree that stood where the church was built. Now, after over 200 years of service, the pulpit is still in use and adds to the purity of the Wilderness Church.

SULLIVAN'S MILL

Silver Dollar City

Near the entrance to Silver Dollar City is Sullivan's Mill. The mill is an actual "turn-of-the century water-powered grist mill," grinding wheat or corn into flour or meal, just as it would have in the 1880s. Sullivan's Mill originally was on Fall Creek. When Charlie Sullivan retired, some of his relatives moved the mill, including the building, to Silver Dollar City, foreseeing the future of the city. Silver Dollar City is a theme park near Branson.

ROCKBRIDGE MILL

The Rockbridge Mill was built in 1892, and was one of the important structures in Rockbridge, Missouri, which was the county seat of the original Ozark County. The mill soon became a focal point of commerce and trade.

Change and the early 1900s industrial revolution were responsible for the demise of the Rockbridge Mill. The mill ceased operations in the late 1940s, but the old mill still stands and is now a restaurant, but more importantly, one of the top trout fishing locations in the state of Missouri.

JASPER COUNTY COURTHOUSE

Carthage

The Jasper County Courthouse currently standing in Carthage is the second courthouse built there. The first, smaller courthouse was unfortunately burned by rebels during the Civil War.

Today's courthouse is constructed, in a large part, of local Carthage marble in the style of medieval castle architecture.

The town is located on historic Route 66 and the courthouse was listed on the National Register of Historic Places in 1973.

College of the Ozarks

This college is a private, Christian liberal-arts college in southwestern Missouri between Branson and Hollister. Now here's the "unique" part – students must work 15 hours per week to pay off the entire cost of tuition. If they work summers, they pay off their room and board. Work-study is not an option, it is the college's justification for existence. Over 90 percent of College of the Ozarks students graduate debt free.

DRURY UNIVERSITY

Drury University is a private liberal arts university in Springfield, Missouri. Originally the school's name was Springfield College. Springfield College became Drury, honoring Samuel Drury's recently deceased son. Samuel Drury was a major donor to the construction of the college's first building. On September 25, 1873, Drury opened its doors and classes began. Drury College became Drury University on January 1, 2000.

PAYNE STEWART

Born in Springfield, Missouri, Payne Stewart began playing golf at the age of four. His father, having been a Missouri State Amateur champion, was his instructor and mentor.

Payne Stewart was well known not only for his golfing career, but also for his wardrobe. He wore "tam o'shanter caps and patterned trousers, which were a cross between plus fours and knickerbockers." Photographers adored him and took his picture often.

At 42, Payne Stewart was killed in an airplane accident on October 25, 1999. This drawing was done from a bronze statue created by sculptor Harry Weber of Wright City, Missouri, for the Sports Hall of Fame.

MISSOURI STATE UNIVERSITY

If you went to Missouri State University in 1905, you would have attended the Fourth District Normal School. If you went to Missouri State University in 1919, you would have been attending Southwest Missouri State Teachers College. A student in 1945 would have been attending Southwest Missouri State College. In 1972, the school became Southwest Missouri State University and in 2006, the university name changed to Missouri State University. Each name change reflected the growing student body as well as programs offered.

Springfield, Missouri is the home of Missouri State University. MSU is the state's second largest university, second only to the University of Missouri, Columbia.

The Alma Mater reflects the attitude students and alumni hold toward Missouri State University: "Sing we praises now to our Alma Mater, all hail maroon and white Missouri State, we pledge devotion… May you live ever in truth and right."

ROUTE 66 SIGN

Well if you ever plan to motor west,
Just take my way, that's the highway that's the best.
Get your kicks on Route sixty-six.

Well it winds from Chicago to LA
More than two-thousand miles all the way.
Get your kicks on Route sixty-six.

… and so it goes, Route 66 originally ran from Chicago, Illinois to Los Angeles, California, cutting a swathe through Missouri, Kansas, Oklahoma, Texas, New Mexico, and Arizona (2,448 miles). Travelling Route 66 was an experience, an "away-from-the-big-city-type experience" with stops at classic little diners. It was such an experience that there was a successful television show and a hit song (a couple of the verses above) that epitomized Route 66.

In 1985, U.S. Route 66 was officially removed from the United States Highway System and was replaced by the Interstate Highway System. Since that time, part of Route 66 has been designated a National Scenic Byway.

KANSAS CITY REGION

This area of Missouri encompasses the west and north west of Missouri, separating Missouri from Kansas. Not only is Kansas City included, but the northern territory that is home to the famous Watkins Woolen Mill, an entire Amish community and Central Missouri University. Northwest Missouri State University hails from this area as well as the retired Star Hill Prairie Hill School near Rockport. The Kansas City area boasts great American history and interestingly is home to one of the Nation's first "shopping centers," the Country Club Plaza. Let's not forget the brief but famous Pony Express that set out from St. Joseph and the museums in St. Joseph. The famous Kansas City Chiefs play in Arrowhead stadium as well as the Kansas City Royals. Numerous other universities are scattered throughout the region and the home of President Harry S Truman is a focal point in Independence. A visit to this area takes days and brings history to life through numerous sites that add to the westward expansion of our nation.

WATKINS WOOLEN MILL

Now a state park, the Watkins three-story woolen mill, elegant home, sawmill, grist mill, orchards, croplands, and more, was a "work-in-progress" for nearly half a century for Waltus Watkins. The Watkins Woolen Mill still stands as a National Historic Landmark. It is the only 19th century textile mill in the United States with its original machinery still intact. Today, the Living History Farm Program makes it possible to see how families in the 1870s lived, worked and played.

Today, in the park there are campsites, playgrounds, places to fish and swim, picnic areas, and opportunities for other fun outside activities. Many of the buildings have been restored, and tours of the Watkins Home and Woolen Mill are given.

Situated in Lawson, Missouri, northeast of Kansas City near Excelsior Spring, Watkins Woolen Mill offers a wonderful piece of history.

Amish Team Horses
"Team Work"

The Amish are very camera-shy, but their horses are not, as John discovered when he asked if he might photograph the three of them working. The farmer replied that his faith did not allow him to be photographed, but that his horses didn't mind. In many farming communities in Missouri, the Amish work the fields using these gentle giants as their power for plowing and harvesting.

University of Central Missouri
Formerly CMSU

In 2005, the Governor of Missouri signed into law a provision authorizing Central Missouri State University in Warrensburg to change its name to the University of Central Missouri.

Over the years, the University of Central Missouri has had many names. Having been founded in 1871, it was State Normal School, then Warrensburg Teachers College. In 1919, its name was changed to Central Missouri State Teachers College; in 1946 Central Missouri State College; and Central Missouri State University in 1971. With each name change came the reflection of the changing nature of the institution.

DOCKERY HALL

University of Central Missouri

The Dockery Hall building stands on the University of Central Missouri's campus. Built in 1905, it withstood a fire in 1915. Dockery Building is a very stately building, perhaps because it was named in honor of Alexander Monroe Dockery. Mr. Dockery took a very active role in Democratic politics and served as Governor of Missouri 1901-1905, Missouri's thirtieth "chief executive."

In 1960, Dockery Hall underwent major renovation, being turned into a classroom facility with four floors. Mr. Dockery died December 26, 1926, but his namesake remains useful, strong, and stately, an integral part of the campus of the University of Central Missouri.

NORTHWEST MISSOURI STATE UNIVERSITY

Maryville

Let your voices loudly ringing,
echo far and near,
Songs of praise thy children singing
to thy mem'ry dear.

Situated in the center of the Northwest Missouri campus, the Memorial Bell Tower stands proudly with the University Seal (which is also the Missouri state seal) in the base of the tower. Tradition dictates, if you walk across the base you risk flunking. It is expected that all should walk around the seal rather than over it, out of respect for the institution. The tower was funded by alumni contributions.

AMERICAN FLAG BARN
Maryville

It just simply doesn't get any more Americana than this – a good old barn that has seen many a day decorated and displaying proudly an American Flag! Yes indeed, think how proud that barn is, being host to one of the most respected symbols of freedom.

Amish Buggy

Jamesport

Jamesport, Missouri is a small town in the northwestern part of the state. This buggy is representative of the Amish community that settled the area and town in the 1950s after the town began to fade from the departing railroad.

Star Hill Prairie School

Rockport

Webster describes "loess" as "a fine-grained, yellowish-brown, extremely fertile loam deposited mainly by the wind and found widely in North America…" and "loam" as a rich soil composed of clay, sand, and some organic matter…." All of the above can be found in abundance on the Star Hill Prairie School Conservation Area, adjacent to the Missouri River floodplain.

Many years ago this area supported a small one-room school, Star Hill Prairie School, near Rockport, Missouri. Time does have a way of marching on, thus the school is gone and this drawing was rendered from very old photos. However, the same area on which it once stood is now a place of dry prairies on ridge tops. It also provides, according to the Missouri Species of Conservation Concern Checklist, "habitat for 12 plant species and two animal species" on that checklist.

Lewis and Clark camped in the vicinity of these rugged loess hills on their journey up the Missouri River. This area now provides a variety of habitats for a number of rare and endangered plants and animals.

Lime Kiln

The importance and use of limestone harks back to early times. It was used in building mortars and as a stabilizer in floors. Kilns that "cooked" the lime were prevalent across the state where lime was quarried.

Today, lime is a key ingredient in the making of cement. Small kilns virtually don't exist; however, some of the foundations live on, such as this one near Louisiana, Missouri.

Round Barn

The height of the round barn construction was from 1880-1920. Early agricultural colleges began advocating round barns "based on the principles of industrial efficiency," plus it was cheaper to construct than styles previously constructed such as square or rectangular. It was also felt that the round layout made it more efficient in that the farmers could work in a "continuous direction." The disadvantage however, was that the round barn was more complicated to build. As machinery became more available and sophisticated, the popularity of the round barn began to fade. It has never been considered a standard barn; however, many round barns still stand today, such as this one drawn by John.

Buchanan County Courthouse

St. Joseph

In 1846, the people of Buchanan County voted to move the county seat from Sparta to St. Joseph. The land for the site of the courthouse was donated and Lewis Stigers's design for a temple-type courthouse was accepted. The work was finished in 1847.

Less than 25 years later, the same architect-builder, Lewis Stiger, regrettably reported that "the building in its present condition is dangerous and unsafe and unfit for the purpose for which it is used." The building had to be vacated in 1871.

Citizens of Buchanan County demanded a new and larger structure. They were presented with an "important and rare example of courthouse design from this period of Missouri's architectural history." The brick structure is trimmed with cut stone, three porticoes project from facades, peaked with a dome 40 feet in circumference. The dome was destroyed by fire and was altered a bit in reconstruction. However, the Buchanan County Courthouse has been placed on the National Register of Historic Places.

Patee House Museum

St. Joseph

This National Historical Landmark originally held the offices of the Pony Express in the luxurious 140-room hotel that served St. Joseph from the opening of the Pony Express until the death of Jesse James. Over the years it was a hotel three times, a U.S. Provost Office, a girls college, a shirt factory and an epileptic sanitarium. Today, it serves as a museum.

PONY EXPRESS STABLES

St. Joseph

The Pike's Peak Stables, as the stables were named, are listed on the National Register of Historic Places, having been of such significance to the Pony Express. The stables are now a Pony Express Museum in St. Joseph, Missouri.

PONY EXPRESS RIDER

The life-size bronze sculpture honors that famous overland mail service by horseback that began on April 3, 1860 and ended October 1861. Relay riders rode between St. Joseph, Missouri and Sacramento, California, covering 2,000 miles in just ten days, delivering and collecting mail at numerous points along the way. Artist Hermon NacNeil created this 7,200-pound sculpture and the St. Joseph Civic Organization unveiled it on April 20, 1940. The Pony Express was another important part of our westward expansion.

St. Joseph Museum

There are several museums in St. Joseph, but the St. Joseph Museum is the oldest, having its beginning in 1927. In 2005, the St. Joseph Museum moved to its new home and is known for its extensive Native American collection. The Lewis and Clark Expedition is featured in the Museum, including heavily their journey through northwest Missouri.

Park University

Park University is in Parkville, Missouri. Both the city and the university are named after Colonel George S. Park. Colonel Park purchased the land and established the city of Parkville in 1838. Colonel Park and Dr. John A. McAfee together established Park College. Colonel Park donated the land and Dr. McAfee recruited students.

On a work/study program, students built Mackay Hall and Scott Observatory in the 1890s. These two structures are still standing on the campus. Colonel Park's 1840 home also remains on the campus. In 2000, Park College was renamed Park University. Park University is built on beautiful bluffs overlooking Kansas City and the Missouri River.

WENTWORTH MILITARY ACADEMY

Lexington

A Mr. Stephen G. Wentworth purchased Hobson's Select School for Boys (founded in 1880) in Lexington, Missouri, and renamed the school in honor of his deceased son, William. The purpose of the Academy "was to prepare its graduates for college and professional life." That mission remains unchanged and now applies to young women as well as men.

Wentworth Military Academy and College is a private four-year college preparatory high school and military junior college. It is the oldest military academy west of the Mississippi River, and the campus is on the National Register of Historic Places.

McCORMICK DISTILLERY

Weston

Ben Holliday was "an enterprising businessman" who lived in Weston, Missouri. He saw the value of the local limestone springs and began selling water to the wagon trains that passed through the Weston area. It wasn't long until Holliday realized that the spring water would be perfect for making whiskey. He built a distillery and made whiskey until prohibition brought it to an immediate halt.

The timeline: In 1894, George Shawhan purchased the distillery and the name then became Shawhan Distillery. In 1936, Shawhan sold the distillery to the Singer brothers and the name became Old Weston Distillery. The McCormick name, used by another distillery in nearby Waldron, was purchased by the Singers and still graces the distillery's labels today. In 1950, Cloud Cray of Midwest Grain Products purchased the distillery.

In 1976, McCormick Distillery was listed on the National Register of Historic Places and was recognized as the oldest distillery in the county still operating at its original location.

THE SCOUT STATUE

This statue dubbed "Scout" was actually passing through Kansas City on its way east, after having won a gold medal at the Panama Pacific Exposition in San Francisco. Scout is more than ten feet tall and stands proudly overlooking downtown Kansas City. On its way home from San Francisco, it went on temporary exhibition in Kansas City. Kansas Citians became so enamored with the statue, that funds were raised and Scout was purchased and this Sioux Indian on horseback pointing east was dedicated in 1922 as a permanent memorial to local Indian tribes.

The next time you're in Seville, Spain, you might want to check out Scout's almost identical twin. However, Seville's statue is pointing in the direction of Kansas City (its "sister city"); the two point to each other. Scout now sits in Penn Valley Park in downtown Kansas City.

COUNTRY CLUB PLAZA
Kansas City

Jesse Clyde Nichols had a dream, and in 1907 he began to fulfill that dream. Many called the project "Nichols' Folly." He began purchasing land for the Country Club Plaza, "the first shopping center in the world designed to accommodate shoppers arriving by automobile." The plaza opened in 1923! "Nichols' Folly" was immediately successful and was no longer referred to as a "folly," but noted by a land developer in the book, *Community Building: The life & Legacy of J.C. Nichols*, that

the Country Club Plaza has had the longest life of any planned shopping center in the history of the world.

The Project for Public Spaces lists the Country Club Plaza in its list, "60 of the World's Great Places." J.C. Nichols had a dream. He transformed land that had been a swamp, land that had no appeal, into the country's first shopping center, the Country Club Plaza.

KANSAS CITY PLAZA TOWER

The Spanish influence on the architectural features of the Plaza are reflected in this clock tower that looms over the shopping area. A timeless piece of this famous area.

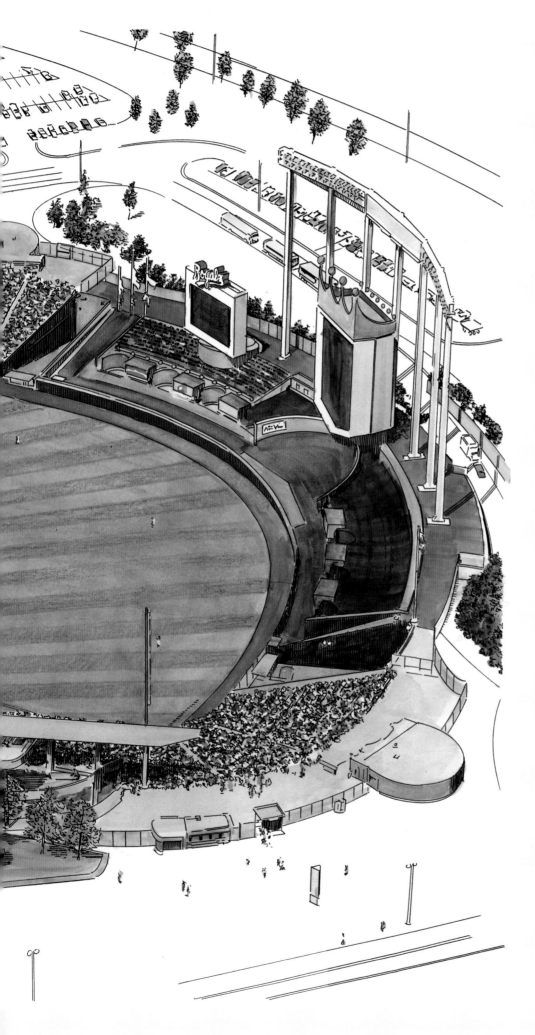

KAUFFMAN STADIUM
Kansas City

Kauffman Stadium was built as and remains a "baseball-only park." It is one of only two such facilities, having never converted for use as multi-purpose. Kauffman Stadium has two view-levels, but most of the seats are on the first level, which puts fans on that level close to the play. All of the seats are now blue, of course, representing the Royals.

The Stadium park's most familiar feature is the fountain and waterfall display behind the right-field fence, dubbed "Water Spectacular."

After the approval of Jackson County voters, renovation of the complex began on Kauffman Stadium on October 3, 2007, being completed for Opening Day in 2009. As part of the renovation, one seat behind home plate was painted red. That red seat is in honor of Buck O'Neil, who was a manager in Negro league baseball. He later became a Kansas City Royals scout. A person is selected every game from community nominees to sit in that Buck O'Neil red seat in an otherwise sea of blue seats!

ARROWHEAD STADIUM

The artist's rendition of Arrowhead Stadium is prior to the major renovation of the stadium. August 12, 1972 was the date of the first game played at Arrowhead Stadium. After some 35 years, with the cooperation of the Jackson County, Missouri taxpaers, the state of Missouri, and the Lamar Hunt family's contribution (Lamar Hunt being the Kansas City Chiefs founder), major improvements began on August 22, 2007. By that time, other facilities having been established in the early 1970s were considered obsolete.

These imporovements made the Truman Sports Complex once again one of the nation's most exciting places to enjoy collegiate or NFL football. First and foremost, however, Arrowhead Stadium is THE HOME OF THE CHIEFS!

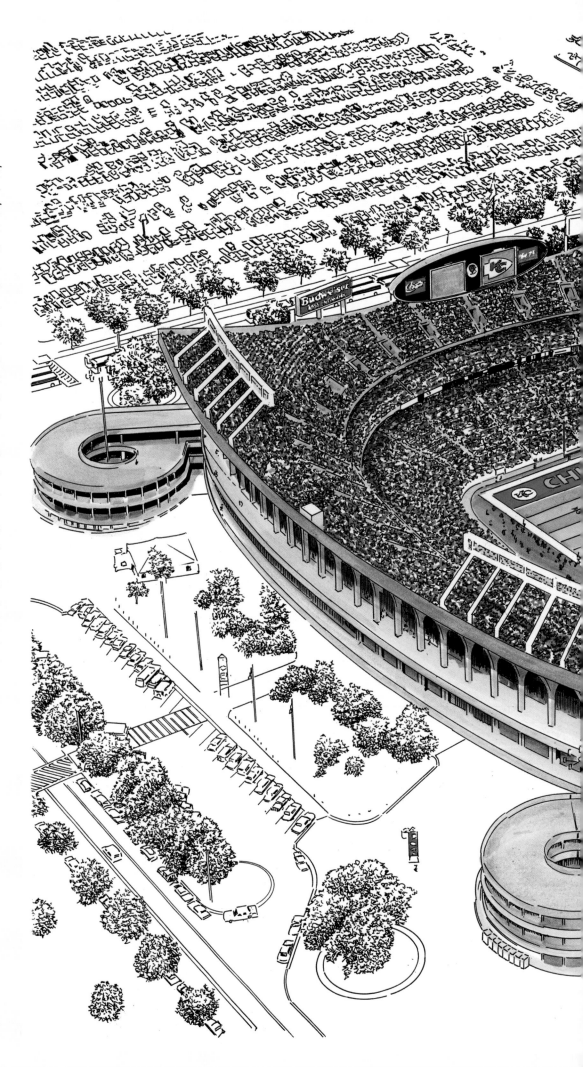

J.C. Nichols Memorial Fountain
Kansas City

The J.C. Nichols Memorial Fountain is a "signature landmark" among the fountains in Kansas City. The Nichols Fountain, erected in 1960 and dedicated to the memory of J.C. Nichols, the developer of the Country Club Plaza, is the best known and most photographed of all the fountains in Kansas City.

The J.C. Nichols Memorial Fountain has four equestrian figures that are said to represent four rivers: the Mississippi River (the one with the Indian riding the horse and beating off an alligator), the Volga River (with the bear), the Seine and Rhine Rivers. Water sprays 30 feet up from the center of the J.C. Nichols Memorial Fountain.

National World War I Liberty Memorial

The Liberty Memorial in Kansas City, Missouri has a congressional designation as the "National Memorial." The 217-foot memorial was dedicated on November 11, 1926, eight years after the end of the World War I. President Calvin Coolidge delivered the dedication speech.

The Liberty Memorial towers 250 feet above a hilltop in Kansas City and it is "the nation's biggest monument to the people who fought in the 'War to End all Wars.'" Within a relatively recent addition of a museum, there is a glass bridge crossing a field of 9,000 artificial poppy blooms, each one representing a thousand soldiers killed in World War I. When one glances at this field of poppies, emotions rise and the realization of the tragedy of war becomes poignant. On September 21, 2006, the Secretary of the Interior declared the memorial a National Historic Landmark.

Both the World War I War Memorial and the monument are managed by a non-profit organization in cooperation with the Kansas City Board of Parks and Recreation Commissioners.

WILLIAM JEWELL COLLEGE
Liberty

William Jewell College is located in Liberty, Missouri. Dr. William Jewell donated a great deal of money to start this Baptist school. William Jewell College is listed among the oldest colleges west of the Mississippi River. It has been named as a national liberal arts college by the Carnegie Foundation for the Advancement of Teaching.

An interesting sidenote, one of the civic leaders and members of the Missouri Baptist Convention who founded William Jewell College in 1849 was Robert James, a Baptist minister and father of the infamous Frank and Jesse James of the James Gang.

ROCKHURST UNIVERSITY
Kansas City

Rockhurst University is in the cultural district of Kansas City. Rockhurst University began as a college. When Missouri chartered Rockhurst College in 1910, also included in the "package" was a high school, Rockhurst High School. The college and the high school remained under the same corporation, but Rockhurst High School moved to its own campus in 1962. Another change took place in 1969 when Rockhurst became coeducational. In 1999, Rockhurst College became Rockhurst University, offering graduate and undergraduate degrees.

What has not changed at Rockhurst University is the fact that it is a private Jesuit university. The school's motto is etched in the stone of the campus bell tower: "Learning, Leadership, and Service in the Jesuit Tradition." Many opportunities are made available for the students to follow its Catholic, Jesuit tradition. There are daily masses, student masses every Sunday evening, and student-led faith-sharing groups.

HARRY TRUMAN STATUE

Independence

This statue is dedicated to Missouri's favorite son, Harry S Truman. Truman was born in Lamar in 1890 and moved to Independence six years later. His statue now stands outside the historic courthouse on the square in Independence, Missouri. The base of the statue reads, "Harry S Truman, 1884-1972, President of the United States, 1945-1953."

While looking at the statue of Harry S Truman, one can almost hear him: "If you can't stand the heat, get out of the kitchen." Gilbert Franklin of Providence, Rhode Island, was the sculptor who created the statue. On May 8, 1976, President Gerald R. Ford dedicated the statue and also celebrated the bicentennial of the United States. Notice there is no period after Harry's middle initial. "S" is actually Harry's middle name, due to the fact his mother did not want to shortchange grandfathers on either side of the family, whose names both began with "S".

HARRY TRUMAN HOME

Independence

To date, Harry S Truman is the only Missourian elected President of the United States. Initially he became President when Franklin Roosevelt passed away while holding the office. He is credited with closing World War II with the atomic bombing of Japan, as well as engaging our troops in the Korean War. President Truman was a personal friend of Winston Churchill, and together they encouraged the creation of the United Nations.

While the birthplace of Harry S Truman was Lamar, Missouri, the home in Independence is probably the most famous as his residence. The house actually belonged to his wife, Bess Wallace Truman, and today is a national site. Truman spoke longingly of this modest Victorian home when he was in Washington D.C., and eagerly looked forward to his return trips to Independence.

THE CREATIVE PROCESS

My work is pen and ink with watercolor. Although some of the drawings are executed on site, most are created in the studio working from my reference photography. People often ask, "How long does it take to do a drawing?" The fact is, they take a long time. A typical drawing, like the Dillard Mill, may take as much as 20 hours to create; a long time to work on site. I have found that I am well served to go to the site when the sun is low in the sky either to my left or right. This will give me reference photography with strong lights and darks. Much thought and creativity go into the photo shoot. I essentially compose the drawing with the camera.

The drawings start as quick thumbnail pencil sketches and are refined to a final rough composition drawing, blocking in the major design elements. Then the pen and ink work begins. At this point, I lay in the significant defining lines; structural outline, architectural features, horizon and tree lines and perspective, all with the final composition in mind. Not until this work is complete do I begin to put the detail, texture, and shading into the artwork. I work one area at a time to completion, rather than bringing the overall drawing forward simultaneously. This goes against the conventional wisdom that one should work the entire drawing throughout the process. At a point near the end, I will step back and evaluate the work overall and make appropriate adjustments. It is during this step that I push more darks into the drawing, taking some areas all the way to black. The addition of these areas of black expands the grayscale all the way from white to black. Without the black, the drawing will lack depth and contrast.

Upon completion of a pen and ink drawing, I will mask the borders of the image and tape the paper to a board to keep it flat during the watercolor work. I use quality tube watercolor paint in my pallet of 24 compartments, blending my colors on the pallet center. Traditional watercolor techniques are followed, working from light to dark, lying transparent glazes one over another to reach the desired effects.

I feel blessed to have a career doing what I love to do and have it come naturally to me. I encourage all to experience the joy of working in your choice of medium. Don't expect to be proficient at the beginning. Like most things in life, there is a learning process. I have learned first, through observing other artists' pen, ink and watercolor work. Seeing how others solve challenges and create visual solutions shortcuts the learning curve, otherwise it's a trial and error process. The materials are affordable. The time spent is a joy. Get started!

ABOUT THE ARTIST

John is a very prolific artist, having created over 400 works of art since 1990, when he left 30 years of corporate life and exchanged his briefcase for his art portfolio and drawing board. His dream to earn a living from his art was a desire he had long held on to during his career in marketing in the Chicago corporate life.

Having graduated from Indiana University in 1966, he moved directly to Chicago with the R.R. Donnelley and Sons Company as an account executive. This introduction to the printing industry and the various types of printing peaked his interest in creating his own limited edition fine art prints. Over the years he created various works of art in different mediums, including sculpture, oils, serigraph silk screens, and pastels. At one point he developed a business plan to create a body of work of silk screen prints for the wholesale art market. But family responsibilities keep him at the security of the corporate desk, and dust collected on the business plan.

In 1985, John moved his family to rural Missouri to assume the responsibilities of V.P. of Marketing for Stark Bros. Nurseries in Louisiana, Missouri. A short five years later the company fell on hard times and, while John had nearly doubled sales, his position was eliminated as a means to save the cash drain. John left the offices that fateful day and announced the time had arrived to pursue his dream of his career in art. The business plan was pulled out of the file, dusted off and revisited.

Twenty years later, the business of John's art does not look anything like the original plan. The original plan was put into action when John created a body of work of 25 decorative serigraphs for the wholesale market. But it was an election year and one of the worse business years in the national art market history. John's work was beautiful, but not selling, and the market continued to shrink. Meanwhile corporate headhunters were knocking on his front door and corporate positions were beginning to look attractive again.

As fate would have it, one sunny day John had gone to Hannibal to have his wife's car worked on and decided to spend the afternoon drawing the Mark Twain Boyhood Home while waiting for the car. Observing from the second floor of the Boyhood Home Museum was Henry Sweets, the curator of the museum. He quietly slipped out of the building and watched over John's shoulder as the image of the house took life on the drawing board. The rest is, as they say, history. The drawing was unveiled at Mark Twain's birthday party at the museum later that summer and John began his art career right in the backyard of his adopted state.

Traveling to all the corners of Missouri, John has visited hundreds of sites and developed them into stunning works of art, publishing them in limited editions for many to enjoy in homes and offices across the state and nationally as well as in many foreign countries. In addition to hundreds of private commissions he has drawn for families and businesses, his work is owned by significant international private collectors, such as Prince Andrew Duke of York, Arch Bishop Desmond Tu Tu, Oprah Winfery, a private resident of the Vatican, the Commander U.S. Naval Fleet Pacific, an F.B.I. Director, a foreign Air Force Museum and Olympic medal winner Jackie Joiner Kersey.

The recipient of numerous awards over the last twenty years for his outstanding works of art, John still prefers to keep his profile low and continue to create what he loves most; work for the homes of just regular folks. Many pieces of John's work are given as gifts and he enjoys hearing of the happiness it brings to the recipient on Christmas morning, birthdays, graduations and other special occasions. A somewhat emotional being, John usually tears up when he hears of the joy people display when receiving one of his drawings.

John's artistic talent was evident at a very early age and he attributes his continued interest in art to a teacher who made all the needed materials available to him to be creative. While still in high school he attended summer workshop art classes at Indiana University, one of which took him to Brown County, Indiana, home of numerous American artists who had formed an art colony in the area. He was highly influenced by one particular artist, Curry Bhome, whose work depicted the local countryside as well as summer studies he did in New England along the coast. During his college years, while majoring in business, John took as many fine art classes as his elective schedule would allow. Coming from a very conservative Midwest family, being an artist was simply not an option as a career. Once settled in Chicago, John enrolled in the Art Institute for evening classes to continue his desire to create while working in his corporate position.

The earliest pen and ink drawings were just that; pen and ink; a clean black line on white paper that gave shape, intense detail and dimension to each site being developed. As time went on John began to add just a touch of color to his drawings. Today most all of John's work is in full color with warm, glowing sunsets or sunrises and each seasons unique and special colors bursting from the paper. The images selected for this book reflect the evolution of his work over the last twenty years.

Just a few years after the famous Boyhood Home drawing, John had created a significant body of work and was fortunate to be asked by the National Park Service to present a display of his works in the rotunda of the Old Courthouse in St. Louis. This was when the title for his collection was born; Reflections of Missouri. His fame, professional abilities and talent were now known in the region and his work became sought after by many. He opened a small gallery in old town St. Charles in the summer of 1995 and had a presence on the street for many years.

His home gallery in Louisiana is in what is purported to be the old stage coach depot built around 1865. Here he continues to draw, paint and frame his works for the various art shows he attends each year, as well as for the gallery.

John and his wife, Karen, have four sons between them. John has one son, Reed, by his first marriage and Karen has two, Aaron and Denton, and together they have one son, Clark, who is also a successful artist. While they are empty nesters (the boys return home for holidays and summer visits), they still enjoy the tranquility of their country home. Frequent visits to Southern France prompted John to build a regulation Bouche court just outside their house, where they spend numerous early mornings in good hearted competition. Artist friends as well as others visit and play this foreign game and enjoy the fresh country air and good Missouri wines that Karen sells at their Eaglesnest winery, bistro and inn in the town of Louisiana. John has created a miniature Brown County environment here at their home, Meadowcrest, and invites other artists to come and enjoy pleinair painting of the countryside, as well as Karen's culinary delights from the kitchen.

Index